My Lips Are Sealed

SUSAN MULCAHY

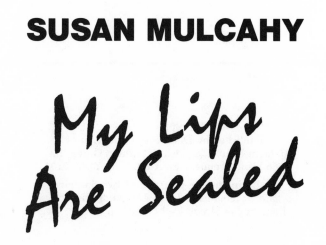

My Lips Are Sealed

CONFESSIONS OF A GOSSIP COLUMNIST

A Dolphin Book

Doubleday

NEW YORK   LONDON   TORONTO   SYDNEY

A Dolphin Book
Published by Doubleday, a division of
Bantam Doubleday Dell Publishing Group, Inc.,
666 Fifth Avenue, New York, New York 10103

Dolphin and the portrayal of two dolphins
are trademarks of Doubleday, a division of
Bantam Doubleday Dell Publishing Group, Inc.

Library of Congress Cataloging-in-Publication Data

Mulcahy, Susan.
My lips are sealed.

"A Dolphin book."
1. Mulcahy, Susan. 2. Gossip columnists—United States—
Biography. 3. Editors—United States—Biography.
4. American newspapers—Sections, columns, etc.—Gossip.
5. Celebrities—United States—Anecdotes, facetiae, satire, etc.
6. Gossip in mass media—United States.   I. Title.
PN4874.M79A3   1988   791.43'092'4 [B]   87-33213
ISBN 0-385-24359-6

BG

For all the unnamed sources.
You know who you are.

ACKNOWLEDGMENTS

Many thanks to those who, through recollection or suggestion, helped in the completion of this book, including Jim Brady, John Cotter, Myron Rushetzky, David Hirshey, Hal Davis, Deborah Orin, Diana Maychick, Richard Johnson, Ruth Hunter, Stephen Silverman, Peter Newman and Antonia Dauphin. Also, thanks to all past and present gossip column collaborators, who were helpful, whether they knew it or not.

Gratitude to my agent, Al Lowman, and my editor Paul Bresnick.

At the *Post,* thanks to my editors, especially Joe Rabinovich and Roger Wood. Also, profuse thanks to the staff of the library there for years of uncredited contributions to the accuracy of gossip, especially Christopher Bowen, and also Billy Heller, Mary McGeary, Faigi Rosenthal, Rick Frazier, Jack Begg, David Hacker, and Merrill Sherr.

At *Newsday,* I am grateful to Don Forst and Tony Marro for granting me a leave of absence to write this book. Extra thanks to Karen Freifeld, Michael Fleming and Jim Revson for filling the space so that no one noticed I was missing for three months. In the *Newsday* library, thanks to Karen von Rossem and Christine Baird for research aid.

For the fact that a (mostly) functioning word processor was used to write this book, I owe thanks to Tony Weiner, Brian Haggler and Ben Kubasik.

And to my family, Jeanne and Paul, Pat, Jo, Chrissy, Nick and Matt, thanks for everything.

CONTENTS

My Lips Are Sealed

Chapter 1

HIGH SOCIETY HORROR AT SEA

At Catholic grammar school, when the "What do you want to be when you grow up?" issue arose, I didn't have a ready response. Nurse and cowgirl were two possibilities. Then, for a brief time, after falling under the spell of the convent classic *Bernie Becomes a Nun,* I contemplated acquiring a habit. The perks, which could include color TV and wall-to-wall carpeting, were inviting. Ultimately, the haircuts sent me seeking some other profession.

No one ever said to me, "Why don't you become a gossip columnist?" For some reason, it wasn't on the list of careers to contemplate. In retrospect, offered this option, I don't know what I would have responded. It would have depended on the presentation. The profession could have been described to me like this: "You will move to New York and get a job at a major metropolitan newspaper. Plaid jumpers, knee socks and beanies will no longer figure in your wardrobe and you will seek more scintillating sartorial statements. Observing the actions of the rich and famous will be part of the work, as will travel. You will be required to journey to Washington where you will brush up against Ronald and Nancy Reagan, Estée Lauder, Ginger Rogers and other staunch supporters of the Republic at inaugural balls, and to Los Angeles, where, at Academy Awards parties, you will share the ladies' room with Michael Jackson one year, and wait on line for the unisex rest room with Farrah Fawcett and Laurence Olivier the next. Film festivals in France will be part of this career package. People like Liz Taylor and Debbie Reynolds will attend these festivals, with their hairdressers. You won't come equipped with a hairdresser, but you'll be drinking so much champagne you won't even notice."

If the possibility of laboring in the gossip vineyards had been couched in those terms, the convent, carpeted or not, wouldn't have held the same allure. On the inevitable other hand, the future might have been sketched in this fashion: "You will move to New York and get a job at a major metropolitan newspaper. There will be many Australians and Englishmen working at this newspaper and whenever you make a mistake they will raise their voices and refer to you as a 'bloody wanker.' You will be required to unearth sensational information about the rich and famous—much of it information the rich and famous would rather not see in print. When competitors like Liz Smith or Suzy unearth more sensational information than you, you will be referred to as a 'bloody stupid wanker.' Some of these rich and famous people will call and complain about your stories. Some will call you things much worse than 'bloody stupid wanker.' At some point, you will feel compelled to retreat to the confessional: 'Bless me, Father, it's been nine or ten years since my last confession. I'm not sure just how many times I've sinned, but I think it may have been unnecessary to question the color of Dan Rather's hair. My CBS sources swear he touches it up, but what if it really is just the lighting on the new set?' "

Faced with this scenario, I might have been tempted to slip into a habit, curl up on the carpet and tune into something colorful.

As it happened, my English grades were higher than those for catechism, so I decided to write. I wasn't sure what I'd end up writing, but I vowed it would be sensitive and important and, once the movie deal had been made, it would ensure my presence at the Academy Awards.

I eventually made it to the Academy Awards, but not as the kind of writer I'd envisioned. I doubt there are any gossip columnists who as tiny tots aspired to a potentially poisoned pen. There certainly isn't any place to train to be one. There are schools of journalism for newspaper reporters, but there aren't any schools for scandal. During discussions of the relative merits of various colleges and universities, no one ever remarks: "I understand they have an excellent gossip department."

It can be argued, however, that all news is gossip. After becoming a gossip columnist, I mastered this form of argument. A story on the front page of a newspaper revealing a rift between the President and his chief of staff, attributed to unnamed "White House sources," is in some ways no different from a gossip item about marital discord between the now divorced Johnny and Joanna Carson: "Is the wedded bliss of Johnny and Joanna blissful no more? Tinseltown types say the marriage is kaput."

The same reportorial skills required of other journalism jobs are also part of writing a gossip column. It is the information itself, and its presentation, that places it in a separate category. The subject matter concerns celebrities, and is often of a highly personal nature.

This information usually is imparted to the columnist in

a clandestine manner, preceded by remarks like "You didn't hear it from me" or "I'm not your source on this."

Bearing prodigious quantities of secretly divulged information can be a burden. It can make the gossip columnist feel like one of those leather things Spanish people are forever filling with red wine in Ernest Hemingway stories. If news flows forth at the proper moment, a scoop is scored. But if the container is bloated and overloaded, and springs a leak at an inopportune instant, reputations may be stained—not a pretty prospect.

On the job, I report stories that have come to me from hopefully reliable sources and have been verified, but off duty, I'm a lousy gossip. If I start blabbing about things told to me completely "off-the-record" and not for publication, and they are spread around, they might turn up in another gossip column, which simply wouldn't do. As Dmitri Karamazov said of one of his brothers: "Ivan's a tomb."

An important part of being a gossip columnist is differentiating between that which is fodder for the column, and that which should stay sealed forever in the vault of unprintable items. This distinction is more difficult to make than it initially would seem, and is tied to the playing of a role.

At social events attended in the line of work, I am playing gossip columnist, which is a schizophrenic part. I'm not really a reporter, in that I haven't been assigned to cover a specific news event, like the aftermath of an ax murder or a speech by a politician. Then again, I'm not really a guest. I receive formal invitations, but I don't receive them on the basis of my achievements in astrophysics or oil painting. At some of these events, I'm aware of a tacit understanding prohibiting the reporting of certain things. Actually, I can write whatever I please, but without the reins of tacit understanding, these events would be one-time-only affairs.

Not long after I officially became a gossip columnist in 1983, I was invited to a party on the *Highlander*, a luxurious yacht owned by multimillionaire publisher Malcolm Forbes. It was the first time I'd been on a boat trip around Manhattan since my first week in New York as a college student. Freshman orientation activities included an evening cruise on the Circle Line. During that ride, several kegs of beer were consumed, after which several of my classmates threw up, though, fortunately, none on me.

Nine years had passed between the two nautical excursions, and I was still drinking beer. On the *Highlander*, the passengers weren't students. They were people like William Paley of CBS, Tom Brokaw and Bryant Gumbel of NBC, author Tom Wolfe, Warner Communications chief Drew Lewis and Delaware's then Governor Pierre du Pont. They may have been drinking beer as well; it was hard to tell. Suffice it to say, whatever they were drinking, it was not out of the plastic cups I recalled from the earlier voyage. And if passengers felt queasy, they could discreetly retreat to the lower deck, where there were several bedrooms, each about the size of my entire apartment, each with its own lavishly appointed bathroom.

I didn't know very many of these people. I was acquainted with Malcolm Forbes and most of his family, it was true, and I also knew Andy Warhol, but I couldn't find him. Women clad in cruise wear—or what I assumed was cruise wear—glided by. Men in somber suits floated from one discussion to another. I wasn't wearing the proper clothes, and I had absolutely nothing relevant to say about anything. On the verge of panic, I yearned for

17

escape, but there was no earthbound exit, no discreet door through which I could stealthily slip away from the indescribable terror of approaching strangers, famous strangers, and making cocktail conversation. A swim to shore appealed.

I knew I would have to strike up a conversation with someone, soon, but I wasn't sure with whom. I considered staying in the corner near the bar to chat with the guy pouring the drinks when one of Malcolm Forbes's sons came over to rescue me. He suggested we walk around the boat and he'd introduce me to a few people. His suggestion made sense. I wasn't going to gain a full perspective on the party if I talked only to the bartender, and diving off the boat would have created an unseemly commotion.

We approached Tom Armstrong, the director of New York's Whitney Museum, and Jerry Zipkin. I should have been acquainted with Jerry Zipkin—often referred to as "The Social Moth"—but I wasn't. The petulant "Walker to the Stars," Zipkin is the frequent escort and confidante to too-thin-and-too-rich women like Betsy Bloomingdale, and Nancy Reagan. He's also supposed to be an incredible gossip, the kind from whom I probably could have picked up a few pointers. I was introduced as being "with the New York *Post.*"

The balding Zipkin, who resembled a well-fed and well-groomed Buddha, minus, perhaps, the spiritual conscience, looked me over and sniffed. It wasn't the sort of sniff I would have associated with narcotics, or nasal congestion. It was a snuff sort of sniff. I wouldn't have been surprised had Zipkin dipped into a hidden pocket and pulled forth a lacquered snuff box. He didn't. "The *Post,*" Zipkin haughtily sniffed again. "Do you write for it, or deliver it?"

18

Suddenly, I experienced a sinking sensation. It wasn't the boat.

No, I didn't deliver the *Post,* but I once had been a paper girl for a newspaper in suburban Philadelphia. Maybe Zipkin had been a subscriber, or a visitor to a subscriber. Maybe he'd been in one of the houses with a front porch my imprecise aim never reached. Maybe he'd been around on one of the occasions when the weight of the paper bag caused me to fall off my bike. Or maybe he just thought I looked like I belonged in the delivery end of the business.

At another party in New York, this time on dry land, I was seated between an actor and an agent. The agent was commenting upon the extramarital indiscretions of another actor, who was with his wife at an adjoining table. I wish I could report what was said, but I don't like "blind" items (those that relate intriguing bits and pieces of the sordid details without naming names), and if I reported the actual discussion, I'd probably be sued for libel, and then excommunicated. It was that kind of a conversation.

In any case, I didn't have to worry about the information passing over my plate, because I wasn't playing gossip columnist at this particular party. I was a regular person. I hadn't been invited by the hosts, but by a friend who'd asked me to accompany him. In those sorts of situations, I often wish I could make a general announcement at the outset:

"I'd like to introduce myself. I'm a gossip columnist, but I'm not covering this party so you can say whatever you want and I assure you I won't write it down and put it in the paper."

Something tells me that this kind of frankness would cause even greater distress than anonymity. As it is, I wait for the questions:

"What is it you said you do?"

"I didn't, but I write a column for a newspaper."

"Isn't that interesting. What kind of column?"

"It's a featurey sort of column."

"Featurey? What kind of features?"

"Oh, you know. People features. Stories about celebrities."

"Well, now, I don't know if you'll find this insulting—but is it a gossip column?"

"You could call it that. I don't find it insulting at all."

"I see. Isn't that interesting. Now what happened to my husband? I'd better go and find him."

Only half the people I talk to at dinner parties react in this fashion. The other half want to know four things:

1. How did you get into that line of work?
2. Where do you get your stories?
3. What's the latest dirt?
4. Why don't you write a story about me?

My party patter responses are:

1. I just, sort of, stumbled into it.
2. I just, sort of, stumble into them.
3. I don't know. Got any?
4. (Silence.)

Even when I am invited as a columnist, I make my own rules for behavior. The most important is: don't use any information that could lead to untimely death, particularly your own. When someone unloads a newsworthy remark, I might comment: "Gee, I write a newspaper column and that would make a good story." If the unloader of the newsworthy information says, "Check it out, but don't say who told you," I have the makings of a story. But, in some cases, the reaction will be more violent, as in: "If you print that story, you'll blow the entire deal, and if

20

you do that, I'll kill you." To statements like that, I respond: "No problem. I don't even remember what you said."

It's not necessary to question the drop of all news items. Each and every one requires its own judgment call. As a child, I listened to countless recitals of my parents' Rules for Clean and Catholic Living, which include the following: "Listening in on phone conversations and reading other people's mail are two of the most despicable things a person can do."

I've attempted to apply this maxim to behavior at parties, where drawing the line between newsworthy information that is fair game and that which will cause undue grief and aggravation if publicized is the most difficult. I may have lost a story or two along the line, but, to the best of my knowledge, I've never committed a mortal sin at a social gathering.

Social dilemmas involving my line of work have led me to dread parties. To be truthful, I've always dreaded parties, but as a columnist, I've had good reason. Part of the dread comes from wondering whether I'll be completely out of my element, and worrying that someone, like Jerry Zipkin, will wonder aloud the same thing: "Who let her in?"

The other part of my party apprehensions revolves around guilt that I should be doing something more meaningful. Try as I might, I am unable to make a correlation between the social work involved in gathering gossip column material, and the other kind of social work. I know I shouldn't bitch. I could be starving, or digging ditches, or waitressing.

Actually, writing a gossip column is a lot like waitressing, which was one of the ways I made money between the paper route and the gossip column. Tips are essential to both disciplines, though with waitressing, each experience presumably ends with a tip, while a tip is just the beginning of a column item. The special vocabulary for each differs, yet certain key expressions convey similar sentiments:

"Yo, 86 fried clams."

"Yo, spike the Mick Jagger story."

Patrons of each have individual tastes. As the couple in the booth against the window will request chutney with their cheeseburgers, so the reader in Brooklyn will demand a little Vladimir Horowitz with his Frank Sinatra: "Enough already about Frank Sinatra. Why don't you people ever write about Vladimir Horowitz? Is it true he's bi?"

The jump from waitressing to column writing was a major one because of the difference in station size. I seldom worked a restaurant station of more than ten tables. When I was writing Page Six, a gossip column in the New York *Post,* the newspaper's daily circulation was close to a million. That's a lot of customers hungry for dish.

Filling that many plates with stories about people who are famous and important is a challenge, particularly when you don't know anyone, let alone anyone famous or important, which was my situation when I started at the *Post* in the spring of 1978.

A twenty-one-year-old senior at Barnard College in New York City, I had one semester to complete the following fall before earning a BA in English. My plan for the summer was to return to Philadelphia, and a lucrative waitressing job. A classmate who was working at the *Post* as a clerk suggested I try out as a copy girl. Though the pay, about $170 a week, wasn't up to restaurant standards, curiosity led me to take the job. I was only a copy girl for two months, distinguishing myself by keeping the coffee orders straight and the rim clean.

The layers of grime on the rim—the semicircular desk where copy editors sat—made me nauseous, so I brought in a sponge and some Mr. Clean and began giving it regular wipe-downs. As the entire newsroom of the *Post* was covered with impenetrable layers of grime, my actions were noticed.

"You the one who washes the rim?" a reporter named A. Cabell Bruce III said to me one day after I'd been at the *Post* for a couple of months. "I hear you're not too stupid. You want to work on Page Six?"

At that time, Page Six, the *Post's* infamously bitchy gossip column, was being edited by Claudia Cohen; Cabell Bruce was the reporter who worked with her. They needed an assistant. At first, I hesitated, wary of Claudia Cohen's reputation as a difficult boss. Then I conducted a financial investigation. The assistant on Page Six made $100 more per week than the average copy girl. Call me crass. Call me material. I did it for the money, and because I thought it would be amusing—for a few months.

Four and a half years later, I was the editor of Page Six, a job I held for three years before moving to New York *Newsday* and a column called "Inside New York." Is this a dignified way to make a living? No. Is this an entertaining way to make a living? Yes. And it sure beats waitressing.

Never having read the *Post* before working there, I was astounded I hadn't discovered it sooner. Not only did its pages contain Page Six, but they were also home to Earl Wilson, dean of show business columnists. How I survived till then without regular updates on the doings of

Earl ("That's Earl, brother.") and his B.W. (Beautiful Wife) remains a mystery.

An avid reader of *People* magazine, I eagerly awaited its nourishing nuggets of information, but they were doled out on a somewhat sparing, weekly basis. Once I began consuming the *Post,* and its rival New York tabloid, the *Daily News,* my diet evolved into daily feasts: Were John Travolta and Liza Minnelli dating? Would Charlene Tilton overcome yet another personal crisis? Did Rod Stewart intend to marry Alana Hamilton?

As I prepared to begin the Page Six job, I tried to imagine what it would be like to meet the hordes of celebrities about whom I'd be writing. I assumed these sorts of encounters would be enjoyable. Until that point, at least, my experiences in the celebrity realm had been pleasant, if relatively uneventful.

One day, while walking across Columbia University's College Walk, I observed Dustin Hoffman shooting a scene for *Marathon Man.* His face was orange. I assumed it was makeup.

In an unrelated incident several months later, I spotted one of Hoffman's co-stars in the film, Roy Scheider, in the crowd at a Manhattan movie theater. And, while working at a small restaurant on the West Side, I waited on a soap opera actress. Her name escapes me, but the bartender insisted she was a big star. Prior to moving to New York, my celebrity experience was confined to an encounter with hockey players Bobby Clarke and Don Saleski, both with the Philadelphia Flyers. They appeared one day at a Howard Johnson's where I was working at the take-out counter. Clarke ordered a chocolate milkshake; Saleski a black-and-white. They tipped big.

Once I started working for Page Six, I imagined, the tips

would be even more monumental. I'd stroll into cocktail parties and start talking to famous people who would immediately unburden themselves of dozens of stories—the kind the city desk would attempt to steal and place on the front page of the paper.

At the Forbes party, I didn't pick up any tips. I also failed to utter a witty rejoinder to Jerry Zipkin. Eventually, I found Andy Warhol.

Warhol had decided my life lacked a certain something. What I really needed was a wealthy husband. A very wealthy husband.

"I think you should go for Bill Paley."

"Andy, give me a break. He's about sixty years older than me."

"But he's sooooo rich. All the girls want him, you know. You better move fast."

Ignoring my protests, Warhol maneuvered us right behind the then-retired CBS chairman on line for the buffet supper being served on the yacht.

"Let's get him to give us a ride uptown afterwards," Warhol whispered.

I don't remember how the dinner conversation started, but Warhol managed to steer it around to post-yacht activities. He told Paley we would be going uptown to a party on Park Avenue and asked him to join us. Paley said he really didn't think he was up for further socializing. But, he added, he would be traveling in that direction and would be delighted to give us a ride in his car.

"You'll make your move in the limo," Warhol advised, *sotto voce.*

Another party sounded like a good idea, as did transportation in a limo, but I can't say I was real enthusiastic about attacking an octogenarian on the way there.

No attacks took place during the ride. When we arrived at the building where the party was being held, Paley suddenly decided he'd come along with us.

I don't know what occasion prompted the party. Perhaps it was just a party for the sake of a party. The hostess was Marina Schiano, a very tall, very flamboyant Italian woman then working with Calvin Klein.

"Daarlings!" she greeted us. "Daarling Andy! Daarling Bill! Daarling Susan!"

Calvin Klein was there, and Steve Rubell, former co-owner of Studio 54, along with several people who'd also been at the Forbes party, including writer Fran Lebowitz and Princess Gloria von Thurn und Taxis. The princess, whose husband is one of the richest men in Germany, had not yet entered her outrageous phase—which would include spiky punk hairdos and suggestive dancing on tables at chic parties—but she was on the way. On this particular occasion, she was dressed demurely, but was performing outrageous, and fairly accurate, imitations of some of the guests on the boat.

Before long, I was uncomfortable. Even though I'd come with Warhol, I wasn't really an invited guest. Was I on the job? I wasn't sure. If I wasn't, what was I doing there? Ah, for the days when going to a party was going to a party, and nothing more. It was getting late anyway, so I decided to call it a night. Warhol approached:

"What happened to Bill?"

"I don't know. I thought he was with you."

"Oh no. I thought you were watching him. He's gone. I can't believe you let him slip out. You blew your big chance."

I don't believe in blowing chances. Things come up— like the Page Six job—and you take a chance on them.

Maybe it works out, maybe not, but you'll never know if another chance might have been the one you blew because you didn't take it. Fairly straightforward logic. If I'd taken a chance on that waitressing job in Philadelphia, I might own the restaurant by now, or at least be head waitress.

A few weeks after the yacht party, I was on the subway downtown to South Street, where the *Post*'s offices are located. Next to me in the crowded car was a familiar face, Maurice Shroder, who had been a professor in Barnard's French department.

We exchanged greetings, then he asked what I was doing. I told him I was working for the *Post*. He said he thought that sounded like fun and asked what kind of writing I was doing. I said, well, actually, I was writing a gossip column.

"Not Page Six?" he asked.

"Yes, Page Six."

Shroder laughed very loudly. "Well," he said, "I guess somebody's got to do it."

Chapter 2

DEAD IRANIANS DUMPED
IN POWER PLAY

It was April 1979 and Claudia Cohen was away on vacation, leaving me and Cabell Bruce to man the gossip fort. Cabell aspired to "serious" journalism. Page Six was but a way station for him, a place to catch his breath, and check out a few interesting parties, before striding into the world of foreign correspondents and investigative reporters. This "gossip crap," in his words, was strictly temporary. It wouldn't be long before he'd be uncovering political scandals and analyzing Third World governments in disarray. I called him "Ace."

Cabell was very well connected. One of the Bruces—as in the late David, former U.S. ambassador to England, West Germany and France, and his widow, Washington society's Evangeline—Cabell, through family connections, was friendly with the Kennedys and a host of other impressive names. He favored the tough guy approach to reporting, which included taking no nonsense from story subjects and using lots of four-letter words. Because he'd been raised in Paris, Cabell's profanity was tempered by frequent lapses into flawless French. One minute he'd be on the phone letting some hapless secretary have it: "The name's Bruce, Cabell Bruce. You tell your boss he'd better come up with a fucking comment before 5 p.m., or else." The next call would be from one of his brothers, leading Cabell to launch into mellifluously Gallic tones.

While Claudia was gone, Cabell had decided, we would seize the opportunity to make our mark with An Important Story. Through diplomatic sources, Cabell had come upon information concerning Amir Abbas Hoveida, who'd served as Prime Minister of Iran from 1965 to 1977, and whose brother, Fereydoun Hoveida, Iran's ambassador to the UN, was known for hosting star-studded New York parties. After the Ayatollah Khomeini took power, Hoveida, once right-hand man to the Shah, was executed. Cabell's story concerned the mysterious disappearance of Hoveida's body from a morgue in Tehran.

Though certainly a news story of some sort, I thought the missing Iranian corpse might be questionable as Page Six copy. I raised the question with Cabell. He wasn't in the mood for questions: "What do you mean, not our kind of story? It's a good, serious story. It's a fucking great story." Well, it was, at least, a story—something long enough to fill the lead space at the top of the page. I certainly didn't have anything more appropriate to offer. The story ran, with the headline: "Hoveida's body vanishes in Iran." A piece on a cozy reunion between Sammy Davis, Jr., and Kim Novak at a Hollywood party, and one on race car driver Mario Andretti signing a deal to write his autobiography, "described as the Italian 'Roots,' " were among the other stories in the column the same day.

The next morning, Roger Wood, then the *Post*'s executive editor, strolled into our offices, located in one of two feature department rooms just off the *Post*'s city desk area.

About fifteen other people shared the space, most of them from the entertainment section—music, theater, film, TV.

A Rupert Murdoch import from London, Wood resembled a rumpled Oxford don. Dressed in brown, he would amble about the office, looking dour and British. When something amused him, he'd grin: "Heh, heh. That's a good one."

He was probably in the latter frame of mind as he entered our office that morning, though his expression indicated the former. "Dear girl," he said sternly as he approached. I was convinced Wood didn't know my name at that point, but even if he had, his comments to those of the female persuasion always were prefaced by "Dear girl," or "Lovely one."

"Dear girl," said Wood. "Do you think we might have some live bodies on the page tomorrow?" He turned to Cabell: "Young Bruce? Some flesh and blood, perhaps of a living sort? We want the column to be amusing and lively. Dead Iranians are neither amusing nor lively."

He turned and walked out. Cabell began muttering obscenities, picking up the phone and slamming it down several times in succession: "Nobody around this fucking place knows a fucking good story when they fucking see one."

"Ace," I said. "He didn't say he didn't think it was a good story. He just said he didn't think it was a Page Six story."

I wondered if other sorts of Iranians were fit for the column? Were only dead Iranians off-limits?

Not until I'd been working on a gossip column for a couple of years, did I give any serious thought to what comprises a successful one. Though I didn't aspire to the same kind of career as Cabell, I did plan to move eventually to some other form of writing. The column was a phase, a diversion, something that simultaneously would pay the rent and prove entertaining. I was convinced I would stay only six months or so, but when six months ended, I gave myself another six—and then another.

Whatever assignments came my way, I attempted to complete, but rarely lingered thoughtfully on story ideas that worked, or on those that didn't. The column usually contained nine to twelve items, a considerable amount of copy to compile on a daily basis. There wasn't much time for reflection. If asked to describe the column, I would respond "short, funny stories about celebrities."

Some time later, an editor from the *Post* who liked the occasional cocktail, the more frequent the occasions the better, called me aside early in the day to discuss the content of the column.

"We need more power," he informed me, sending potent waves of gin-scented breath in my direction.

We definitely needed a lot of power, I agreed, taking a deep breath as I volunteered to run right back to my desk and begin a search for some.

"Hold on," he detained me. "Do you know what I'm saying? There isn't enough power in the column."

Was it the writing he found wimpy, I wondered, or the subject matter? Slightly light-headed myself from inhaling such noxious material at so early an hour, I wasn't sure.

"We need more power stories," he declared. "For instance, who's New York's power dentist?"

My own dentist seemed unlikely to qualify—the only person I'd ever recognized in the waiting room was another reporter from the *Post*—but I had no other dental contacts.

"Who's New York's power optometrist?" he continued. "Who's the power surgeon? You've got to know these things!"

Would I be ordered to write a series of stories on root canals of the rich and famous, or one on myopic movie stars? Celebrity cyst removals?

Though my ability to wash a desk was undisputed when I started working on Page Six, I seemed to lack other qualifications needed to work at the gossip trade. First of all, I had never heard of half the people we were writing about. Raquel Welch, Ted Kennedy, Princess Grace—they fit my concept of celebrity. Page Six covered not only those sorts of notables, but also business and media tycoons, political consultants and others of a behind-the-scenes ilk.

Laurence Tisch was the primary power at Loews. Richard Snyder ran Simon & Schuster. Sam Lefrak owned a lot of buildings. I'd never heard of any of these guys, and wondered if knowledge of them was necessary to leading a full and balanced existence.

Apparently yes, because whenever Claudia would assign a story, and I would say "Who's that?" she would roll her eyes upward and moan, "I don't believe it. Don't you read the papers?" I had started, but apparently had some catching up to do.

Eager to avoid being perceived as ignorant, I stopped asking "Who's that?" and began relying on the *Post*'s library. Whenever Claudia would tell me to check out something, I would express an urge to go to the ladies' room, which was located past the city room, near the end of a hall at the opposite end of the building. At the very end of the hall was the library. If I had called the library's staff on the phone seeking identification of someone whose renown was unknown to me, Claudia, who sat to my left, would have heard, and all would have been lost. Instead, I walked there myself, and began to depend on the library's staff and on its rows of wooden cabinets containing small manila envelopes filled with newspaper clips.

The walk also offered a glimpse of the city room in action. Mostly a collection of broken-down desks and chairs, and even more broken-down manual typewriters, the city room resembled a huge ashtray. Everyone smoked, and used the floor to extinguish cigarettes or cigars. At day's end, the more inveterate chain smokers would be seated next to piles of smoldering butts. The only savory thing about the *Post*'s offices then was the view.

On South Street in a six-story structure that once housed William Randolph Hearst's *Journal-American*, the *Post* has magnificent views of the East River and the Brooklyn Bridge. The sight of the latter proves particularly useful to the *Post* in beating the other papers on "jumper" stories.

Every several months, someone spots a human figure on the bridge—one of New York's more popular suicide spots —poised and ready to plunge. Photographers and reporters spring into action, rushing out for a picture and, hopefully, an "exclusive, moments before death" interview.

If the would-be jumper is talked down by the police, an air of disappointment pervades the city desk, in the knowledge that a dramatic "Death Leap!" headline has been lost.

I made many trips to the library. Screwing up fact checking might have spelled unemployment. Though I viewed the Page Six experience as an experiment—figuring I could always return to my copy girl's job in the event of a disaster—modernization of the *Post*'s operation quickly killed that notion. About six weeks after I joined the Page Six staff, the *Post* switched from the traditional "hot" type to "cold" or computerized type. Numerous jobs were lost in the transition to the new system, including the position I'd held as a copy girl on the rim.

I barely knew how to type, and learning the quieter computer keyboard made the job easier in that it kept this fact hidden from Claudia. It didn't help in identifying what constituted a suitable item for Page Six, however. The column has its own identity, as do each of the other New York gossip columns. Comprehending the intricacies of said identities is not an overnight process.

The contents of a gossip column traditionally reflect the tastes of the person writing it. The most personal gossip columns are those associated with a single individual, like Liz Smith, Suzy, William Norwich or Cindy Adams, written in the first person and featuring a photo of the columnist at the top of the copy. The photos are very small and usually are changed only when the columnist undergoes a drastic alteration of hairstyle. These columnists are the descendants of Walter Winchell, Cholly Knickerbocker, Louella Parsons and Hedda Hopper.

Page Six was one of the first of a new, less personal, breed, born after Watergate altered the process of all journalism, including that involving celebrities. There are no photos at the top of Page Six, or New York *Newsday*'s "Inside New York," giving those who write them the freedom to alter appearance with frequent and wanton abandon. These columns are written in the third person, as in "insiders inform us" or "Page Six has learned," lending the material the air of a news story. Part of the impersonal nature of these columns emerges from the fact that they are compiled by teams. Not only do an editor, a reporter and an assistant work on Page Six, but reporters from other sections of the newspaper contribute to it as well. The situation is similar at "Inside New York."

In fact, Page Six, started when Rupert Murdoch bought the *Post* from Dorothy Schiff in 1976, was designed partially as a showcase for material from other parts of the paper, for amusing information that might not fit in a regular news story or for material that a particular reporter would like to see published, but not with his or her name on it, for fear of alienating a contact, or revealing a source. For instance, if the City Hall bureau chief has a good friend/source in the mayor's office, the friend/source may be marked as a leak for a certain type of inside story if the bureau chief's name appears on it. If it is printed in Page Six, the tie to the bureau chief won't be as obvious. Also, if the story is a negative one, the mayor won't fire the friend/source, enabling the friend/source to continue to leak with impunity, like the proverbial sieve/source.

The layout of a column also contributes to its profile. On any given day, the standard, first-person gossip column will cover several different stories, written in column form, with each one running into the next, but on occasion it may be devoted to a single topic—be it the unfolding of a new romance, or a play-by-play account of a particularly momentous social occasion.

Gossip column aficionados remember with relish the seventy-fifth birthday party of multimillionaire Henry (Jack) Heinz, tossed by his loving wife Drue in 1983. Suzy, then covering the social beat for the *Daily News,* was so summarily blown away by the bash, she devoted four days' worth of columns to it. With each installment, new names were added to the sparkling guest list, and new dishes to the mouth-watering menu. By the time the coverage ended, *Daily News* readers, even those living in reduced circumstances, felt a certain intimacy with Drue and Jack, and, indeed, were surprised that they too hadn't been invited to the party. But with Suzy's slavish attention to detail, it wasn't even necessary to leave the house: "The specially made tablecloths were of rustic hopsacking, dyed wheat-color, the napkins were cream linen teatowels decorated with tiny silk-screen print tomatoes and rolled and tied with silk tomato leaves and vines . . . Surrounding the colanders were dozens of vegetables so tiny as to be almost unborn." Considerate of her readers, she saved them the time and effort, not to mention the expense of a gift for Jack.

The format of a gossip column like Page Six is much more rigid, with each item placed separately on the page under its own headline. The editor of Page Six might have had one hell of a time at Drue and Jack's, but would have been able to devote only one space to the party, and might not have had room to mention the tea towels, let alone the baby vegetables. Seven to ten short pieces appear in the column each day, two of those topped off by a small photo—a closely cropped head shot of the story subject. There are two longer stories as well. The longer piece at the bottom of the page is referred to as the double column, the one running across the top as the lead. The lead space is supposed to be filled with the meatiest story of the day, the most important of the items. (That, assuredly, is where an account of Drue and Jack's party would have been placed.) But there are plenty of days when nothing important occurs. On those days, the lead position is taken by whatever's available, the blanks filled in with background material from clips.

Page Six and "Inside New York" differ from some of the other gossip columns in that they trade in both serious and ridiculous information. Because of their formats, there is room to mingle fluff with material of more substance. During the time I edited Page Six, any number of "serious" stories were broken there, including a piece on Mobil Oil's boycott of *The Wall Street Journal,* and the story of Pulitzer Prize-winning journalist Sydney Schanberg's conflict with, and departure from, the New York *Times.*

The column was also the first to write about Bess Myerson, New York City's Commissioner of Cultural Affairs, hiring as her assistant the daughter of State Supreme Court Justice Hortense Gabel, then presiding over the divorce of Myerson's boyfriend Carl "Andy" Capasso. Soon after the hiring of Gabel's daughter by Myerson in 1983, Capasso's alimony and child support payments were reduced. In October 1987, after lengthy investigations by city and federal officials, Myerson and Gabel, both of whom were forced to leave their jobs, and Capasso, were indicted by a federal grand jury. The charges against Myerson included conspiracy and obstruction of justice.

We also were first with more typically gossipy information, like Jerry Hall's pregnancy with her first child by Mick Jagger, and the romances between Caroline Kennedy and Edwin Schlossberg, Sean Penn and Madonna, and Billy Joel and Christie Brinkley.

Ever hopeful that the Pulitzer Prize people someday will recognize gossip columns as a reputable part of the journalism industry, I point to the so-called serious stories when someone asks, "What were your biggest scoops?" But, if Pulitzers were handed out according to reader interest, Caroline and Ed, or Sean and Madonna, would win hands down.

Page Six-like columns are now commonplace, as the shortened attention spans of generations weaned on television favor brief news items over full-length stories. Page Six was not the first to offer news in this format, but its popularity was a harbinger of the rise of junk food journalism. When *USA Today* first appeared on national newsstands, the staff of Page Six was quite flattered, as we viewed it as an entire newspaper based on the Page Six format. We focused our brief items on the personalities extruded by a constantly churning celebrity machine.

Many of the integral parts of the celebrity journalism machine in operation today were added around the time of Watergate. Prior to that revelatory era, the intimate details of the lives of many currently considered public personalities were neither "widely known" nor "often referred to"—the Webster's definition of "celebrated," as in celebrity. Movie stars have always generated much attention from the media, but not White House attorneys or chiefs of staff.

Once Bob Woodward and Carl Bernstein exposed Richard Nixon and his associates, previously covert thoughts, words and deeds of public personalities became fair game. No longer was there a tacit agreement between politicians and reporters to keep the lid on certain sordid things. If John F. Kennedy were on the scene today, his relationship with Judith Exner would not be under wraps. Neither would that between Dwight Eisenhower and Kay Summersby. It would probably be the subject of a story in the Washington *Post* "Style" section. And if Gary Hart had run for President twenty years ago, he never would have had to face reporters eager for his opinions on adultery.

Watergate's influence extended far beyond Washington. It helped make it possible for anyone—regardless of field of endeavor—to become a celebrity. Woodward and Bernstein became celebrities themselves, portrayed in the film version of their book *All the President's Men* by Robert Redford and Dustin Hoffman. When I was working for Claudia Cohen on Page Six, she urged me and Cabell Bruce to study the Woodward and Bernstein method.

"I want you to go rent that movie," she advised. "And just count how many phone calls they make on a single story." Unfortunately, I didn't have a VCR.

Watergate wasn't solely responsible for opening the floodgates of celebrity, but it made a significant mark on journalism by extending the limits of exposure.

The real exposure came during the congressional hearings—but only because they were televised. Television, with its ability to instantly transform the unknown into the celebrated, has had the greatest influence in forming a perception that anyone can be a celebrity.

In determining which potential stories are worthy of inclusion in a gossip column, there are two factors to consider: who and what. First comes a decision involving the celebrity and whether or not he or she warrants attention. That is a personal decision, although the columnist, through devotion and duty to readers, should take into account the interests of others.

It's not possible for me to watch soap operas—not if I intend to show up at the office—and yet I write frequently, and with false assurance, about Susan Lucci, Eileen Fulton and other stars of suds epics. The ratings on daytime dramas are high, leading me to suspect someone is watching them. Therefore, I probably should be writing about them, and do.

Professional sports also fall beyond my personal interest zone, but, in light of the attention paid to newspaper sports sections, it has occurred to me that gossip column readers might care about people like Ron Darling and Ron Duguay. I find it helpful to have people working with me who are acquainted with the intricacies of sports, thereby avoiding confusion of basketball players with boxers, and vice versa. Even so, mistakes have been made, like the time I referred to Keith Hernandez as Darryl Strawberry's "fellow Yankee," and subsequently was subjected to interoffice disgrace, and reader disdain. One Owen Murphy of the Bronx sent me a letter informing me that he had "several retarded friends," interested in careers in the newspaper business, who all had "severe problems with reading comprehension and no knowledge of Major League baseball"—rendering them eminently qualified to take over my job. He ended his note by inquiring, on behalf of his retarded friends, as to "the name of the fool that hired you." Several weeks later, I attended my first Mets game, noting the names of people wearing Mets uniforms in the hopes that the error would not be repeated.

Still, I do have personal favorites. Tipped off to an item about Mel Gibson, or Menudo, I am one happy columnist. Or Joe Franklin, the venerable New York area late-night talk show host given to observations like "Dead celebrities are still stars" and "Baby, you're a genius. You know why? You called me." I jump at any chance to call Joe for a phone interview. It's important not to overdo it, however, and I attempt to limit Joe Franklin items to one per month.

Once the "who" has been determined, and the celebrity subject of a story has been dubbed interesting, the "what" comes into play.

Suppose the celebrity is Julio Iglesias, certainly a notable worthy of copious comment. Suppose the proposed item involves Iglesias singing at a charity supper. I'd probably pass on an opportunity to cover the event. Lots of singers lend their voices to charity events. It's not unusual, and it's not very interesting. But when Iglesias doesn't sing, as he didn't at the Super Bowl in 1984, it makes an item—the item being that he didn't think he'd be able to remember the lyrics. Barry Manilow warbled "Oh, say can you see" instead.

A gossip column by definition is a mélange of material involving celebrities, but defining celebrity isn't as cut and dry. Wealth and fame are not prerequisites.

On the *Forbes* 400 list of the richest people in America, there are dozens of unfamiliar names. Take John Berry, Sr., the son of the inventor of the Yellow Pages. Berry, who lives in Dayton, Ohio, is worth more than $300 million, but he's hardly a household word, and likely wouldn't have been invited backstage had he attended Liza Minnelli's Carnegie Hall concerts.

To understand the inner workings of the celebrity state, I learned to separate it from fame. An achievement of some sort is necessary for fame. It's possible to be famous and be a celebrity, but there are many for whom the label of celebrity stands as their only genuine accomplishment. They've done absolutely nothing to warrant adulation or acclaim. These are the true celebrity achievers.

Ron Reagan, son of the President, had a brief career as a so-so ballet dancer. He's also been an actor, a free-lance writer, a radio commentator and a regular on "Good Morning America." Admitting he's "not the next Faulkner or any of those names," Ron described his status in an interview as "one of those cheap kinds of celebrity. I didn't go out looking for it, but the machinery feeds on that sort of thing. You're the new hamburger meat or you're the flavor of the month."

Ron Reagan is an ideal gossip column candidate.

The longer I worked on a gossip column, the more striated my mind became on the subject of celebrity, building layer upon layer of personalities fitting the celebrity bill. A list of the celebrity arenas covered by the *Post*'s Page Six or New York *Newsday*'s "Inside New York" would include film, theater, television, politics, business, media, law, sports, book publishing, fashion and society—with both visible and behind-the-scenes figures from all those worlds qualifying as celebrities.

The entertaining celebrities, the "stars" from the world of show business—actors, singers, dancers, musicians— would have been celebrities thirty years ago as well. Some of them, the likes of Liz Taylor and Frank Sinatra, have been written about in columns for that long, or longer, but the way in which they are covered has changed. The coverage has gotten nastier, and more personal. The Kitty Kelley biography of Frank Sinatra probably wouldn't have been published before the rules of journalism were rewritten by Watergate, and the constant commentary on Taylor's weight gains would have been less direct.

The society celebrity also has been around for decades. Just as Brenda Frazier rated reams of copy as "Deb of the Year" in 1938, so Cornelia Guest, whose debhood is endless, has proven a staple of more recent society coverage. The crowned heads of foreign nations, like the Windsors of England or the Grimaldis of Monaco, would have been figures of note in earlier eras. So would sports stars like Chris Evert, Refrigerator Perry and Keith Hernandez—the modern day equivalents of Gussie Moran, Jim Thorpe and

Babe Ruth—only now their high profiles lead to phenom-enally high salaries.

Movie stars, royals, athletes and society types are the rare celebrity constants. Other now commonly covered personalities never would have appeared in the celebrity picture of another time. Fashion designers like Calvin Klein and Ralph Lauren only recently have emerged from behind the racks of Seventh Avenue to become more cele-brated than their clothes. Politicians certainly have been written about in the past—but not with the intensity that they are today, as televised campaign commercials make politicians as familiar as the stars of a network sitcom.

Corporate tycoons, the newest breed of celebrities, have climbed to the top of the celebrity heap as dramatic corpo-rate raids and takeovers—and the equally dramatic crimi-nal indictments of many of those involved in corporate maneuverings—proliferate. Seeing Ronald Perelman and Michel Bergerac slug it out over Revlon was as exciting as watching a juicy episode of "Dynasty."

As the definition of celebrity has expanded, so has its extended family. The daughter or son of a celebrity is a celebrity simply by virtue of the blood tie. The battalions of laborers who perform special services for celebrities—in particular, those services requisite in a picture of the glam-orous, good life—become celebrities themselves. Nancy Reagan's three hairdressers, Monsieur Marc, Julius Bengtsson and Robin Weir, have been the subjects of nu-merous feature articles. So have such exercise trainers as Jake Steinfeld (Body by Jake) in Hollywood or Radu in New York, who cater to the celebrity body beautiful.

With the gates of celebrity standing wide open, al-lowing entrance by everyone from such business person-alities as Lee Iacocca and T. Boone Pickens to figures of notoriety like Claus von Bülow and Sydney Biddle Barrows, material available for gossip columns should abound. It does, but the simultaneous multiplying of these columns has made it harder to land stories considered major news. Even the competition for minutiae is heated.

When I think about some of the stories for which a gossip columnist has to vie, the process seems slightly absurd, not to mention humiliating and humbling.

Once, after being shown a greeting card featuring a photo of Katharine Hepburn, and a notation that it was being used with the actress's "special permission," I decided to try and find out what had lead Hepburn to participate in what was for her an unusual commercial endorsement. I called her representative—an agent, as I recall —and he said I'd have to write a letter to him, which would be forwarded to Hepburn and maybe, eventually, I'd get a response.

I couldn't be bothered with all that. Besides, I had another New York phone number for Hepburn, which I assumed was some sort of office. A very distinct voice answered the phone. It was her home number. I gulped and identified myself, then inquired as to why she had lent her name to a commercial venture.

"What a silly ass thing to be calling me about," said Hepburn. "You make me laugh." She didn't, and hung up the phone.

Though news stories of some importance are carried by gossip columns—and upon occasion, there is material in columns like Page Six and "Inside New York" that actually borders on investigative journalism—there is no denying that much of what fills the space is "silly ass."

Isn't that the point?

Newspaper readers don't turn to gossip columns for

news of peace talks, or editorial opinions on toxic waste disposal. And when news of a summit appears on Page Six, it is usually about what Nancy Reagan and Raisa Gorbachev wore, not what their husbands said.

At the *Post*, I was constantly reminded that stories from "the corridors of power" were to be sought for Page Six— but seldom straight business stories. Preferable were tales of characters from the power-filled corridors immersed in ridiculous predicaments.

The following are condensed versions of several "silly ass" Page Six stories.

1. The carols of Christmas rang discordant for John Gutfreund, chairman of Salomon Brothers, the Wall Street brokerage firm, and his socialite wife Susan, when they became involved in a not-very-jolly seasonal feud with neighbors in their posh East Side co-op. The feud began with a Christmas tree, which the Gutfreunds allegedly sneaked into their apartment using the co-op's roof. The Gutfreunds' neighbors filed a $31 million lawsuit, accusing the couple of "planning and conspiring" to perpetrate "intentional, willful, malicious, wrongful and otherwise corrupt" Yuletide activies involving the tree, an elevator, a Betamax and floral arrangements. It was assumed the arrangements didn't contain any mistletoe.

2. Smoke got in the eyes of skin care expert Janet Sartin on a flight from New York to L.A. The culprit was Robert Mitchum, who was lighting up a cigarette a few rows away. She reminded him he was in a no-smoking section, later noting that smoke is "deadly to your cellular structure." Mitchum crushed the butt out on the arm of his seat, stood up and moved toward Sartin. Then, Sartin reported, the actor turned his back to her, bent over and "let out a rolling burst of wind such as you've never heard in

your life. Then he stood up proudly and looked around."
After the incident, said Sartin, she wasn't able to enjoy
Mitchum's work on screen, not even in the mini-series
"The Winds of War" in which she found him "very dull
. . . expressionless and stilted."

3. The Carter clan had an answer for underprivileged
minorities—designer diapers. During the period when
Jimmy Carter was running the country, his grandchildren
were being used as "test babies," trying out a new product
called "Show-Offs." The disposable diapers, covered with
cutesy kiddie prints, were the brainchild of Georgia-based
Edna Langford, mother of the President's daughter-in-law
Judy Carter. Langford said the throwaways were popular
"in very low-income areas. It's one of the only pretty
things those people have." She also revealed that "the cir-
cus animals, in real bright reds and yellows—they're the
ones that really sell in your black areas and Puerto Rican,
and that sort of thing."

4. Barbara Cartland, the Queen of Romance Novelists,
threw down her white gloves and came out swinging
against a British politician who said he'd once seen Cartland lose a false eyelash. "It spread [down her face] like an
escaped tarantula," said Liberal Party leader David Steel.
Cartland denied all and decried the fact that Steel "should
stoop to tell a cheap lie to get a cheap laugh." It never
could have happened, said Cartland. "My lashes are glued
on so tightly that I have to pull them off at night," she
explained.

No, none of these could be considered "stop the
presses" news, but, then again, the only time I ever heard
anyone yell that famous newspaper phrase at the *Post* was
the day Henry ("The Fonz") Winkler got married and pro-

duction was halted in order to insert the story, with photos, in the paper's late editions.

Gossip is an ephemeral commodity—particularly as it appears in a newspaper. Like unrefrigerated fish, it ages badly.

In 1981, I wrote a lead story about actress Genie Francis. "Hang on to your chairs, soap opera fans. Genie Francis, who stars as Laura on TV's top soaper, ABC's General Hospital, and who is quitting the show at the end of this month, has both CBS and NBC dangling huge money offers under her pretty 19-year-old nose." Did she haul her suds to another network? I guess so, but I don't remember the details, and frankly, who cares?

The same goes for another item from 1981. "Cheryl Tiegs and her longtime chum, jet set photographer Peter Beard, plan to wed Memorial Day weekend in Pete's Montauk home, PAGE SIX has learned." Well, we did have the story first, but since the couple is now divorced and Beard has married again, it's become a moot scoop.

It's the tone that renders gossip items anachronisms—the impression that the information being reported is of great importance or will have great impact. Some of that information will be remembered, but much of the "exclusive" news is now a part of a likely forgotten, and overly detailed, celebrity history.

But an ability to age gracefully doesn't really matter as far as the content of a gossip column is concerned. Nobody asked for *War and Peace*. The details, however variable, are out there, as are readers eager to soak them up.

After a long period of experimentation and observation, I've come to the conclusion that gossip column readers are interested primarily in two categories of celebrity information. The first brings the celebrity down to a human level, often by way of disaster. The disaster might be simply embarrassing, like a weight gain, or the failure to be recognized by a disco doorman. It can be something serious as well, like bankruptcy. The human element also emerges in the telling of tales about celebrities doing everyday things, say, comparing prices of dish detergent at K-Mart.

When Yoko Ono and stepson Julian Lennon, wearing "jeans with patches," were turned away from a restaurant as improperly attired, Page Six ran an item about it. We also carried a short piece about Jackie Onassis being told there were no tickets left to a film event she wanted to attend at Lincoln Center. "If it had been the Pope, we wouldn't have had tickets," said a staffer at the arts center. These stories show that, despite wealth and fame, the celebrities are Regular People, and can be rejected, just like you and me.

The second category of information makes apparent the fact that celebrities are not Regular People at all. This is the "Glamour and Luxury" category. When it was learned that Liz Taylor and Calvin Klein were among those who'd successfully bid vast sums of money for pieces of jewelry once owned by the Duchess of Windsor, it was perfect gossip column material. Taylor may have problems with one type of pounds, but not the British kind, used in purchasing the accessories required of a movie legend. Attending events like the royal wedding of Charles and Diana, or a White House state dinner qualifies as glamorous as well.

Gossip is also about deals. When New York City mayor Ed Koch made a deal to write a book about his experiences, it was a Page Six lead story. Deals that are broken make news too. When Mick Jagger signed a similar agreement to put on paper the sure-to-be-page-turning details of his life, he wasn't able to fulfill his end of the bargain, and it turned into a story of a deal unmade.

Relationships form the personal end of the deal-making spectrum. The start of a celebrity romance is worth writing about, as is a marriage or a divorce.

In the writing of a gossip column, a light touch prevails. My early instructions from Roger Wood to keep things "amusing and lively" were sound. As it is poor news judgment, and often poorer taste, to leaven certain news stories with "fun" writing, those stories will appear in columns like Page Six or "Inside New York" without the addition of any gossipy touches. Often, however, a story that warrants inclusion in some other part of a newspaper will became gossip material simply by virtue of its less straightforward style.

When Texaco filed for reorganization under Chapter 11, the New York *Times* started its story with: "In a case that started as a contract dispute between two oil companies, Texaco Inc. yesterday filed for bankruptcy . . ." If Page Six had broken the story, it might have started with "They're reaching for the Valium in the executive suites at Texaco . . ."

In the fall of 1985, Page Six ran what appeared to be a fairly innocuous item, of the sort press agents attempt to plant, about a celebrity acquiring expensive designer eyeglasses at a store in New York. The celebrity was Daniel Ortega. The headline on the story was "Leninist Lens."

"Daniel Ortega, his wife Rosario and their entourage, protected by a contingent of Secret Service agents, and transported by more than a dozen limos, arrived at Cohen's Fashion Opticals at 60th and Lexington yesterday for some serious shopping. So serious, the entire block was cordoned off. 'I've never seen such a production,' said manager Noel Cottington. The Nicaraguan Marxist leader wanted bulletproof glasses. He bought six pairs with special polycarbonate lenses—a thin, lightweight, indestructible material developed for the space race—at $200 a pair. He bought his wife two pair as well, and got three pair of Fiorucci frames with regular lenses for their daughter. The bill came to $3385."

The story had been planted by a press agent, one of the old school, Jack Tirman, who represented Cohen's and who constantly tried to convince us to run stories about celebrities buying eyeglasses. He talked so fast I could never figure out what he was saying, so I turned over Jack Tirman interpretation duties to Richard Johnson, the reporter then working with me on Page Six. The story probably wouldn't have run if I had spoken to Tirman myself, because I wouldn't have been able to comprehend what he was saying. Johnson did, and we got an entertaining item out of it, and that was that. Or so I thought.

The story was picked up everywhere and proved so powerful a gauge of the Central American political climate that members of the Reagan administration began to refer to Ortega as a "dictator in designer glasses." More than a year later, Ortega's wife Rosario was still answering questions about the spectacle debacle. In an interview with *Vanity Fair* she explained, "I had no idea how much a pair of glasses could cost. I had never been shopping in New York before."

If Ortega had been a dead Nicaraguan, he wouldn't have been suitable Page Six material. But, as a breathing big spender with proletarian pretensions, he was amusing and lively—and ideal gossip column copy.

Chapter 3

CELEB MOM IN BABY WEIGHT SCAM

If only I'd read *Heartburn* back in 1979, I never would have called Nora Ephron in the hospital.

But *Heartburn,* Ephron's autobiographical novel about the breakup of her marriage to Carl Bernstein, had not been written yet because Ephron was still experiencing what would form the basis for the plot—discovering, while pregnant with their second child, that her husband was having an affair.

How was I to know? All I knew was that Ephron had had the baby, Claudia Cohen wanted a quote from her and I was assigned to contact the new mother in the hospital. I was not excited about making the phone call.

Though gossip column items often begin with phrases like "Rumor has it that . . ." or "The word around town is . . ." the information is not unsubstantiated. If columnists simply were to compile pieces of innuendo, the results would be lively reading indeed—and likely libelous. The information has to be verified—facts confirmed and sources double-checked.

Figuring out what constituted a Page Six item was only

one part of the gossip column process, and was followed by a hunt for the big game—an exclusive story.

Some newspapers have official reporter-training programs. At the *Post*, reporters learn on the job from a variety of instructors, ranging from scholarly Upper West Side liberals left over from the days of publisher Dorothy Schiff to manic right-wing Australians hell bent on ridding the world of The Red Menace. I first studied gossip under the tutelage of Claudia Cohen.

Had I stayed in the city room, my reportorial tutors would have fit the description "ink-stained wretches." They would have been chain smokers. They would have worked amid the howls and screams of police and fire radios. At the end of a shift, they would have bolted from the city desk to a local gin mill where they would have bolted back a couple of stiff ones. They would have been consumed by The Big Story: MURDER. MAYHEM. MASSACRE.

Though the Page Six process wasn't all that wildly disparate from the operation at the city desk, Claudia was not your average ink-stained wretch. The daughter of the wealthy owner of a newspaper and magazine distribution company, Claudia did not rely upon her *Post* salary for survival. She often let her paychecks collect for several weeks in the cashier's office until small change was needed; then I would be sent down to fetch them. When Claudia was married a few years ago to Ronald Perelman, the owner of Revlon and other corporate entities, moving her from the ranks of the very rich into those reserved for the indescribably wealthy, my immediate reaction was: is there a limit on the number of fur coats one person is permitted to possess?

Many of my gossip-reporting lessons involved the

phone—answering it, or using it to confirm and elaborate upon information to be used in the column.

Conducting reporting work on the phone has its advantages. Though the subtle touches to be garnered during a personal encounter are missing, so is the face-to-face rage that may pour forth if the person contacted doesn't care to discuss the information being sought. What it boils down to is this: it's less painful to be yelled at over the phone than in person.

Then again, the phone has drawbacks too.

When I was working for Claudia, I often would come into the office in the morning to find scraps of paper left on my desk from the night before—bits of articles ripped out from obscure publications requiring additional information to be expanded into a story, or notes detailing a rumor needing checking. Often, Claudia would call before coming into the office to get me started on stories for the following day's column.

The morning she phoned to tell me Nora Ephron had had her second child, she said I should call the hospital immediately.

Ephron, then thirty-eight, was in Mount Sinai, where she'd just given birth. The baby was seven weeks premature, and I didn't imagine it had been an easy experience. Would she really want to talk to a reporter?

By the time Claudia had arrived at the office, I still hadn't called.

"Was it a boy or a girl?"

"Uh, I haven't called yet."

"Why not? Come on, let's get going."

I wondered why I couldn't just confirm the birth with the hospital and leave it at that, but no, Claudia wanted quotes. I picked up the phone and called patient information. When I got through to Ephron's room, a very groggy voice answered.

"Hullo?"

"Uh, I'm calling from Page Six at the *Post*. We heard you had a baby and we wanted to do a story about it."

(Silence.)

"You guys must be pretty hard up for news."

"Well, uhhmm, I was wondering if it was a boy or a girl?"

This question prompted another pause on her end of the line, then she responded, in a very slow, somewhat pained fashion.

"It's a boy. His name is Max. The kid's okay. I'm okay. Is that enough?"

"Uh, yeh, sure, fine, thanks. Bye."

Claudia had been sitting at her desk observing my technique: "Well?"

"It's a boy. His name is Max."

"How much does he weigh?"

"Shit, I forgot to ask."

"Call her back."

"Claudia, I can't call her back. She sounded sort of sick."

"Then you should have remembered to ask her. We have to know how much the baby weighed. Call her back."

It was at this juncture in my journalistic career that I made a crucial decision. This wasn't nuclear arms we were writing about here. Suppose Ronald Reagan and Mikhail Gorbachev had an argument at a summit meeting, and Reagan said, "Screw you, Gorbachev. I'm going home to tell everybody to speed up weapons production until we have enough to blow you and all your pinko friends sky high." And then, without commenting on this or talking to reporters, he just jumped on a plane for the ranch in California. Taking this hypothetical situation one step further, suppose I had his secret private number at the ranch. I wouldn't hesitate to pick up the phone and give him a buzz, seeking comment and explanation. I wouldn't even care if it was after 10:00 P.M. and he and Nancy already had gone to bed. Even if he'd gotten an earache on the plane from his hearing aid—tough luck, I'd call anyway.

From what I could discern, confirming the fact of birth with the hospital, or Ephron's agent—anybody other than the person lying in a hospital bed—would have been enough. For a story of this sort, the personal touch was completely unnecessary.

Try telling Claudia that.

"Hurry up, call her back while she's still awake."

I picked up the phone, positioning myself so that the instrument of torture was not visible to Claudia. Using one hand to push down the button, I dialed a number with the other. Then I asked for Ephron's room.

"Hi. I forgot to ask you how much the baby weighed. Okay, thanks."

I turned to Claudia, inventing the figure as I did: "Six pounds, four ounces."

"Now was that so hard?"

No. Now I just had to figure out how to get the real weight and then a way to explain to Claudia that the numbers I'd gotten from the mother were wrong. I could always say Ephron was delirious.

As an apprentice, I wasn't given much opportunity to vent my views on the different forms of gossip and which were appropriate to Page Six. The editor of the column made those decisions. I just listened, and dialed.

In the course of tracking down items for a gossip column, a reporter is required to ask some fairly strange questions, about plastic surgery, divorce and other intimate topics. The most common response to these questions is: "I can't believe you're calling about this."

But call you must because those ridiculous, silly, "fun" stories that appear in gossip columns all have to be verifed. Making the calls on the items is nowhere near as much fun as reading them.

When Luci Johnson Nugent and her husband Patrick Nugent were rumored to be on the verge of a divorce, Claudia somehow got their home phone number in Texas and instructed me to call and get a comment, and some juicy details. For several days in a row, I tried, always getting the maid or housekeeper, who told me Mrs. Nugent was out of town. I prayed she would never come back.

At other times, the phone calls would be unnerving because of the personality involved. Take Arthur "Punch" Sulzberger, publisher of the New York *Times*. When Claudia discovered his possessions also included a handgun, she instructed me to give him a ring for a quote. What would I say to the guy who actually owned The Newspaper of Record? "So, Punch, blow anybody away today?" I breathed a sign of relief upon discovering he wasn't in the office that day. All I had to do was chat with his secretary, who said Sulzberger kept the gun for security reasons, but, to the best of her knowledge "He's never had to shoot at anybody."

It was nice to know.

Though Claudia was a very demanding superior, I liked

working at a newspaper and I figured Page Six was as good a place as any to learn how a reporter functioned.

There was one thing I assiduously attempted to avoid: treading on the bad side of the instructor. Claudia's wrath could be formidable.

During the 1978 newspaper strike, when unions at the *Post*, the *Daily News* and the *Times* all took a long walk, Claudia was one of several writers who filled the time with temporary positions on local television stations. Hers entailed reading gossip items on WCBS-TV. Before the start of one of her segments, anchorman Jim Jensen said something Claudia found insulting. She never told me precisely what he had said, but I got the impression it had unnerved her, and she felt he'd done it intentionally. He was not to be forgiven.

Months later, as a dispute involving Jensen's divorce came to court, Claudia got hold of the legal particulars. The day Claudia wrote the first story about the divorce dispute, primarily involving alimony payments, she called her mother in New Jersey. "Mommy," she said, with a note of glee in her voice. "I got him."

Page Six ran several accounts on the dispute between Jensen and his ex-wife, airing whatever dirty linen was available. At one point, enraged at the persistent publicity, Jensen asked the court to seal the file, stating that the newspaper stories "serve no legitimate news function and just are included to appeal to the prurient interest of the Post's readers."

In the middle of the proceedings, Jensen's son was killed in a hang-gliding accident. The stories didn't stop. A line in the next account on Page Six read: "Jim (who in a tragic hang gliding accident recently lost his son) backed off, admitting he owed [his ex-wife] a few bucks."

No, Claudia was not the type of person I wanted to annoy, and rarely did. I knew my place and parked it there, doing what I was expected to do. My tasks often were not what I would have expected.

Once, when Claudia was preparing for a night on the town, she sat before the large, lighted mirror she kept on her desk. After putting on her makeup, she began to undress. Rather than walk all the way down to the ladies' room, Claudia asked me to hold her coat up in front of her so she could change behind it. As it was late, there were only two, maybe three, people still working in our room, but you never knew when a printer or pressman might walk through, or somebody from the city desk. Holding the coat in front of her while she donned her evening clothes, I wondered if Woodward and Bernstein ever had been required to shield Washington *Post* editor Ben Bradlee from prying eyes while he slipped into a tuxedo.

Another stage of gossip education involved the actual writing of the column. Claudia preferred what she referred to as a "Page Six slant," which translated to: insert the knife and twist it around a few times.

One of her stories, about a dieting Elizabeth Taylor, began "Knock off the malted milk balls, Liz." Another started with "These are depressing times for chubbettes who ate too much pasta over the winter. Take Faye Dunaway." And, on Gore Vidal checking into a fat farm: "Enough with the fettucine already, Gore."

Claudia, obviously enthusiastic about celebrity weight gains, attempted to train me in this writing style, which also made use of "kickers," the jabs that end items.

An item on Margaret Trudeau concluded that the former first lady of Canada's "long unawaited autobiography," would be an "insomniac's feast."

A story about former New York City mayor John Lindsay participating in a benefit skating show described him as "no stranger to thin ice" and one on a new pastry chef hired by Monaco's Princess Grace ended with the comment that "Prince Rainier, for one, doesn't need the calories."

Writing aside, the most crucial part of story construction is figuring out the lead. If an item on Pat Robertson contains information about his ministry and his political plans—and also mentions that he and his wife were married a mere ten weeks before the birth of their first child, leading the story with the politics would not be proper gossip column style. "Pat Robertson married shotgun style" is more appropriate to capturing reader interest.

When Claudia's lesson plans failed to inspire, I looked to the city desk for motivation and guidance.

Gruesome news was very big at the *Post,* which took New York tabloid style a step further, adding dashes of Fleet Street after Murdoch took over. "KILL FOR THRILL GRAVEYARD," "GRANNY EXECUTED IN HER PINK PAJAMAS" and the infamous "HEADLESS BODY IN TOPLESS BAR" were typical front-page headlines, accompanied whenever possible by photos of barely dressed models and actresses. The bizarre and the macabre were always worth writing about. As I was passing by the city editor's desk one day, news came through of a plane crash. Excitement mounted, but there were no casualties. "God damn it," he muttered in frustration. "Nobody dead." The city desk was also the first place to hear the latest in topical humor—jokes involving deaths of world leaders, and other newsworthy tragedies.

Though the Australians and other Brits brought in by Murdoch were reputed to be the outrageous ones, many of the Americans who worked at the *Post* were just as entertaining—particularly the staff of the lobster shift, those reporters and editors who worked from around midnight to 8 A.M.

Cy Egan, a reporter who worked lobster, was acclaimed for deadpan deathbed reportorial skills. As it was explained to me: "If there's an execution, they save it for Cy."

Often assigned to interview the families of murder victims, Egan, in a uniquely gravelly voice, would call the mother or sister or husband of the deceased:

"Mrs. Salerno? This is Egan from the *Post.* Your daughter. Can you tell me if she was sexually molested? Were her clothes torn or ripped? Had she been otherwise maimed or multilated?"

Though stiffs missing limbs and bodies riddled with bullet holes only occasionally figured in Page Six assignments, seeking the sensational was still *de rigueur* when constructing a lead.

After several months on the column, I suddenly found myself working alone. It was the day before Thanksgiving, and Claudia had decided to take a long weekend. I'm not sure where Cabell Bruce was, but he wasn't in the office. While visions of turkeys, parades and day-after-Thanksgiving shopping danced in most heads, mine was a void. No items. No sources. No sense of holiday conviviality.

At that time, Page Six paid twenty-five dollars for story tips, both to *Post* staffers and to a select group of outside stringers. Walking out of the drama room, I took a left and headed in the direction of the city desk. Standing before the city editor, I declared: "I'm desperate. Got any items?" It was to become my deadline battle cry.

A couple of reporters came through with stories, but

none suitable for a lead. Then I received a call from Stuart Applebaum, head of publicity for Bantam Books, about a "quickie" book being rushed into print. It focused upon the events of the week before in Guyana—the infamous Jonestown massacre—where more than nine hundred people died, many after being forced to drink poisoned Kool-Aid by leaders of the Peoples Temple sect.

On an average day, news of the book would have been a regular item. This wasn't an average day. I pressed Applebaum for details. Was there any blood, any guts, any sex? Any hope of blood, guts and/or sex?

Thankfully, one of the authors had received numerous death threats and was writing his portion of the book in a secret location. I was ecstatic. Drama and mystery, not to mention the possibility of a maniacal cult member bursting into the writer's lair and attacking him with a deadly weapon, made for a lead story. The headline was "MASSACRE TALE AUTHOR IN HIDING." I was overcome with pride at this journalistic accomplishment.

Never having worked at a newspaper, I assumed the *Post* functioned like any other. Apparently not. To much of the rest of the press, the *Post,* at least in the early years of Rupert Murdoch's stewardship, was an alien environment. Them.

There was no denying that the *Post* was a foreign outpost, and some of its staff strangers in a strange land. I'd never heard of a green card until I started working there. Before long it became clear that if, in my next life, I returned to earth as a British citizen, I would know just what to do in the event of immigration to the United States. One day I had a discussion with an editor about the use of the word "row" in a headline. I said I didn't think New Yorkers defined "row" as "quarrel." I said they probably thought, as I had, that "row" meant an ordered and linear arrangement of objects. He said I was dead wrong, and then he asked me if I knew where the Bronx was.

Even the *Post*'s location is seemingly at the ends of the earth, or at least the very end of Manhattan.

The recent renovation of the South Street Seaport has radically revised that area of lower Manhattan bordering the Brooklyn Bridge, but when I first started working at the *Post*, the neighborhood was more sparsely populated, particularly near the Fulton Fish Market. Patrons of local drinking establishments were often dock workers, who would hang longshoremen's hooks on the bar as they ordered beers.

There is also said to be a Mafia presence in the neighborhood. Bodies sometimes were discovered in the area bordering the building, with at least one rumored to have been a mob hit. Upon occasion, other corpses were spotted in the waters across the street, the "floaters" that are a seasonal surety in New York, as the warmth of spring brings to the surface of the city's rivers a variety of items, including dead bodies, that have been dumped there during the colder months.

DEATH. KILL. HELL. HORROR. TERROR. Inside the building and out, at the city desk and on the gossip column, a theme emerged, and it involved corpses.

One year, at the *Post*'s annual Christmas party, then held in the basement of San Giuseppe, the Catholic Church up the street from the newspaper's offices, I was cornered by Adam "Curly" Brydon, a Murdoch executive.

Prior to that, the Christmas party had been held in the city room. The decision to move it to the church was made following a festive bash during which one of the *Post*'s editors got into a raucous fistfight with someone from accounting. The booze flowed freely. People stood on desks. Drinks were poured into computer terminals. It was the best office party I've ever attended. Things calmed down considerably once we shifted to the House of the Lord, even if it was the basement of the House of the Lord.

Also said to have contributed to the party transfer was a legendary encounter in an elevator between Rupert Murdoch and a couple of smashed *Post* staffers. The next day, a notice was posted prohibiting the consumption of alcoholic beverages on the premises. Those staffers incapable of functioning in any but an inebriated state observed the new rule by carrying their liquids in brown paper bags, and drinking them discreetly from Styrofoam coffee cups.

At the Christmas party, Brydon, known as the Wing Commander (he'd been the Royal Australian Navy's leading air ace during World War II), expressed concern about the direction of the column. "You've got to really give it to 'em," he advised, punching the air in front of him for punctuation. "It's not bitchy enough. Go for the kill."

I tried, but there were those skeptical of my skills. Occasionally, the proper mark would be hit, but my killer instincts never seemed to reach a consistently lethal state. Dejected at this inadequacy, I contemplated retiring. There didn't seem to be a choice. I knew what the Brits would say: "It's for the best. You just don't have it, old girl."

Suddenly, Claudia quit, defecting to the *Daily News.* The moment she walked out the door, her Rolodex under her arm, the gossip lesson plan altered, drastically.

Her successor on Page Six was Murdoch executive Jim

Brady, who several years earlier had devised the Page Six format.

Brady was an easygoing tutor. Though a lead was still a lead, and sensations of all sorts continued to be appropriate copy, one distinct difference entered into his version of the gossip process. Brady was concerned with putting together a column that was amusing to read, but he was more interested in poking fun at celebrities than he was in stabbing them into bloodied pulps. The body count dipped into low digits.

Not one to agonize over the daily process, Brady felt it best to get the column off to press and move on to the next one. The only inefficient thing about Page Six during his tenure was the fact that he refused to learn the computers. Claudia eventually succumbed, but Brady would not be convinced.

"Didn't I hear you screaming yesterday that it had eaten one of your stories?" he would say when informed of the efficiency of technology. "Those machines are ravenous! They are insatiable! I will not submit my prose to their mechanical jaws!"

Brady puzzled me at first. Though he'd mentioned that his brother was a priest, he didn't strike me as a religious zealot. Yet every afternoon, as we were putting the finishing touches on the next day's column, he would roll down his shirt sleeves, put on his suit coat and announce, "Looks like we're in reasonably good shape. I think I'll head up to the chapel."

I continued to be in awe of his spiritual fervor until the day he invited me to join him at the chapel, which turned out to be St. John's, a bar at the corner of Forty-ninth and First. Brady claimed it was a hotbed of information for the column. There was no denying its location provided much Truman Capote grist for the Page Six mill.

Across the street from the chapel was a haircutting establishment run by two Greek immigrants, Mr. Tino and his assistant, Mr. George. Most of the regulars at the chapel were also regulars at Mr. Tino's, as was Truman Capote, who lived in the neighborhood and who also visited the chapel once in a while. At one point, when Mr. Tino and Mr. George had lost their lease and were on the verge of being booted from their quarters, Capote, a creature of habit who didn't want to have to find a new location for his daily shampoo and shave, went door to door, seeking another nearby site for the locks-smiths:

"If you live on E. 49th St. and the door bell rings unexpectedly, it's not Avon, or even the Fuller Brush man—it's Truman Capote."

Page Six ran several stories on the Tiny Terror and the plight of his tress tamers, into which we inserted as many execrable puns as possible.

Brady was interested in non-chapel-related material as well. While Claudia Cohen, who'd once worked at a media magazine, had a special interest in stories pertaining to the press, Brady, though familiar with the ins and outs of that world, was the former publisher of *Women's Wear Daily* and editor and publisher of *Harper's Bazaar,* and was equally interested in fashion and fashion journalism. He told us endless tales about the eccentricities of various designers, and about John Fairchild, the head of Fairchild Publications and the power behind *WWD,* the industry's bible. We heard stories of Coco Chanel's funeral, of the American designer referred to as "Princess Tiny Meat" and of the French designer whose lover was a New York City policeman. Asked how he and the cop amused themselves, the French designer replied: "I wear his hat, then I blow his whistle."

Occasionally, I'd wonder what life might have been like if I hadn't happened into the *Post* and developed an addiction to tabloids. I might have been doing what was expected of a person from a respectable family with a respectable degree in English—laboring as a poorly paid editorial assistant at a politically correct monthly journal. Pathetic, but true, and I'd never even have known what I was missing.

Once an addiction to tabloid journalism develops, it's difficult to kick. Spotting a headline like "MISSING MOM FOUND IN FREEZER," tabloid addicts will stop short at a newsstand and grab for a copy of the paper. If necessary, they will knock small children out of the way, impulsive in their need to know how long the body had been there, and how foul the play involved. Hopefully, there will be photos. A story on Walter Hudson, the 1,000-pound-plus man who hasn't left his house in twenty-seven years, elicits a similar response. Tabloid addicts eat up details of his diet, which includes two pounds of bacon, a dozen eggs, a dozen rolls, jam and coffee. And that's just breakfast. Also appealing is a front-page story about "STAR'S MYSTERY LOVE NEST" or the tale of a famous actress's battle with booze and pills, accompanied by her secrets for staying slim.

At first, before the addiction truly took hold, employment at a tabloid seemed an ill-fitting garment. Shouldn't I have been trying to get a job at the *Times?* Were dead people, fat people and famous people proper topics for serious journalistic endeavor?

Some time after joining the *Post*, I was walking along a street on the Upper West Side when I ran into Sacvan Bercovitch, a professor of English at Columbia University.

In his Puritan Literature class, we'd spent a great deal of time dissecting *The Scarlet Letter.* Upon encountering him, I felt emblazoned with a "G" for gossip. How to explain that I had abandoned the analysis of the pioneer spirit in early American literature, and had moved on to more recent emblems of Americana, like Blake Carrington and J. R. Ewing? It wasn't necessary.

"I heard about your job," he said with surprising enthusiasm. "It sounds terrific. Have you met Jackie Onassis yet?"

Mike Pearl is a reporter who's worked at the *Post* for more than twenty years. A wall near Pearl's desk in the Criminal Courts Building is papered with his favorite headlines, including "300 LB GIANT SEIZED IN SEX ATTACK" "NIGHTMARE IN HOT SHEETS HOTEL" and "SHE WAS NICE TO ME, THEN I KICKED HER OFF THE ROOF." It's known as the "Wall of Shame."

When the Washington *Post* was preparing a feature story on what is becoming a vanishing journalistic breed in the United States, the tabloid, a reporter approached Pearl for his opinions on the essential ingredients.

He responded: "Five things. Violence. Sex. Blood—no, that doesn't count. Money. Kids. Animals. Is that five?" Then it's six—famous people, big names.

Page Six stood slightly apart, and yet fit neatly into the tabloid process at the same time by incorporating not only the big names, but the other five categories as well, as they relate to the big names. There was also a certain amount of figurative blood shed in the hunt for column items.

So what's a little blood? I'd much rather be wounded than kicked off a roof.

Chapter 4

PAUL NEWMAN
DRIVES OFF CLIFF

In early 1984, Ronald Reagan's reelection campaign was seeking an advertising executive to produce its commercials. The front-runner was Madison Avenue's Jerry Della Femina.

For those who'd read a 1981 interview with Della Femina in *Oui* magazine, this came as some surprise. In the interview, he was quoted as saying he had no desire to work with politicians: "I don't sell products that wake up grumpy in the morning and press a button and kill everybody."

He was quoted as discussing other interesting things as well, including an annual "sex contest" at his agency, the prizes for which, he said, included a "Kink Award. Everybody votes for the person they want to commit their kinkiest sex act with." According to *Oui,* when Della Femina won, he said he considered it "the greatest honor I've ever received."

To some, these comments cast Della Femina in a non-GOP light. I thought the interview made Della Femina sound perfect for the Reagan/Bush effort, which could have used a little kink, or at least a little livening up. But when Page Six got hold of a copy of the *Oui* article and ran select excerpts, the Reagan/Bush campaign machinery did not purr. Campaign staffers were late in happening upon the interview, and when they did, eyebrows were raised. The story on Page Six began:

"Required reading at the White House this week: the January 1981 issue of Oui magazine. No, staffers were not ogling the skin pix."

When I called Della Femina for a quote about the *Oui* interview, I was told he hadn't made any of those controversial comments, and that he'd considered suing *Oui* when the article was first published. Later, he did file a lawsuit against the trade publication *Adweek* when it ran a story about the *Oui* controversy. The suit eventually was thrown out of court.

Reagan/Bush didn't hire Della Femina. Campaign aides said it had nothing to do with the *Oui* interview, and was related to a problem with timing. Whatever the reason, the Republicans obviously wished the interview would disappear—particularly from the well-read Page Six.

When I called the Reagan/Bush campaign for a comment on why Della Femina wasn't joining the reelection effort, a press spokesman told me he would rather I didn't run a story about it.

"Oh, c'mon," I said. "Of course I'm going to run a story."

He darkly hinted that it might be difficult to cooperate with Page Six for the remainder of the campaign if I did.

"Is that a threat?" I asked.

"Oh no," he said.

When the press spokesman called back later, he'd dropped the hints, opting for a more blunt approach. He told me that the head of Reagan/Bush '84 would "personally see to it that you are made a hero in Rupert Murdoch's eyes if you play the story right."

Gee whiz, thanks for that little tip, I said, and hung up the phone. Then I wrote the story as I'd originally intended.

Yes, the *Post* is right wing. Very right wing. Murdoch's leanings are conservative, and he's definitely a Reagan supporter, but I really doubt he would have approved of the President's reelection staff recklessly flinging his media weight around.

What part does politics play in a gossip column? A large one. Howard Baker may not smirk as fetchingly as Bruce Willis, but he's got an extra ingredient more entertaining celebrities will never possess: power. And, at the *Post,* reminders were constant that power was an ingredient crucial to successful Page Six stories.

Republican or Democrat, it doesn't make any difference. A rule of thumb for any reputable gossip column is: take no prisoners, of any political or ideological bent. Still, politics is a gray area.

Most newspapers have political biases, and are perceived as conservative, liberal or moderate organs. Even so, when I first started working at a paper, I was under the impression that news was news. Boy, was I ever stupid.

Though I probably haven't gotten any smarter, I'm at least slightly savvier about politics, and its ties to journalism. The relationship is often too close for comfort. The bonds arise partially from the fact that politicians understand the exigencies of ink. It is no accident that many political and government press secretaries are former reporters.

Politicans usually take their knocks more graciously than other subjects of unfavorable news stories. While a movie star, through a press agent, may scream, yell, holler and threaten never to cooperate with a reporter again if something seen as unfair appears, politicians are more pragmatic. They may complain loudly in private, but in public many of them subscribe to the "at least they spelled my name right" theory. Politicians are apt to realize a need for press, while notables from other fields sometimes claim to prefer inattention. There are no Sean Penns among politicians. They tend to sprint toward cameras, rather than away from them.

Though by now I've followed the rise and/or fall of a number of New York politicians, and I know more than a few of them, I wouldn't call any of them close friends. In recent years in New York, watching one politician after another indicted on criminal charges, I've been grateful not to have to write about friends going to court, or jail.

Post gossip columnist Cindy Adams believes in thinking positively. As the number of criminal indictments of city officials was growing almost daily, she threw herself a birthday party. When she called to invite me, she said: "All my friends are coming. Half of them are indicted, but what's the big deal? It'll be fun. My line is: if they're indicted, they're invited."

In New York, one of the more entertaining mingling of politicians and reporters takes place at the annual Inner Circle, a charity dinner that's a must-attend for all New York politicians. The political reporters stage a musical revue, with lyrics altered to reflect the dinner's theme. In 1987, in the midst of the city scandals, the theme was "Greed Lock."

There are actually two Inner Circles—the black-tie event on a Saturday night, attended by politicians, newspaper editors and other bigwigs, and a Friday-night dress rehearsal to which reporters and junior political staffers flock. The Friday-night performance is more lively, but, for a reporter, an invitation to the formal Saturday-night event is considered an honor. I was still an assistant at the *Post* in 1980 when I received an invitation to the latter from a congressman I'd never even met—Fred Richmond of Brooklyn.

I still don't know where his press secretary got my name. Perhaps I had called him on a story involving Richmond, but that wouldn't explain his inviting me rather than the editor or reporter on Page Six. I occupied the column's bottom rung.

The day before the Inner Circle, Richmond's press secretary called to tell me I should meet the congressman at 7 P.M., to accompany him on the rounds of cocktail parties that precede the show and dinner.

At the top of the escalator on the floor where the dinner would take place at the New York Hilton was the designated meeting place. Standing there, I wondered why I had been asked to be, in effect, Richmond's date for that part of the evening. It was a mystery to me.

From room to room, from one party to another, I followed Richmond, who introduced me to everyone, from Mayor Ed Koch to Senator Pat Moynihan, plus most of the city's top newspaper editors and columnists, simply as "Susie." Finally, I saw a familiar face, a friend who worked at City Hall. He started laughing when he saw whom I was with.

"So, you're the beard."

"What beard?"

"The beard, the blonde Fred Richmond is dragging around with him."

"I don't know what you're talking about."

"The beard, the cover. C'mon, don't you know about the little boys?"

If I did, I hadn't made the connection, and had been blind to this possible explanation for my invitation, despite the fact that I was wearing brand-new contact lenses. Richmond, who eventually resigned his congressional seat after pleading guilty to a variety of charges, including tax evasion and drugs, had begun his descent into a scandal-ridden phase that would destroy his career. Some of the scandals involved young men, including a twenty-one-year-old bodybuilder, who two years later would be found dead in Richmond's New York apartment.

Apparently, I was the suitably female ornament for the evening. Suddenly, the entire production was cast in a new light.

Once we reached the table where we would be dining and watching the show, Richmond sat down next to someone else. I looked for an escape route. Across the ballroom was a table occupied by executives and editors from the *Post.* I said I had to go and greet my bosses, and slipped off. At first I'd been flattered by the invitation, but in the wake of this new interpretation for the reason behind it, I felt sort of, well, soiled.

The *Post's* table proved more lively, in any case. While the buckets in the center of most of the ballroom's tables contained two or three bottles of wine or champagne, the one adorning the *Post's* was filled with bottles of beer. The rest of the table was littered with wine bottles.

I pulled up a chair and joined the *Post's* table, at which several of the editors, including Kelvin MacKenzie, an Englishman then running the *Post's* lobster shift, were seated. MacKenzie was placing another order with the waiter:

"Could you bring us seven more bottles of the red, mate, and another dozen beers?"

MacKenzie, now the editor of Murdoch's racy London *Sun,* a newspaper that makes the *Post* look like the *Ladies' Home Journal,* was the composer of many of the paper's infamous front-page headlines in an era some consider the golden age of screaming woods. (The wood is a tabloid's front-page headline.) When several rock concert fans were killed at a Who concert, MacKenzie's wood was "ELEVEN DEAD AND THE BAND PLAYED ON." MacKenzie's favorite expression was "toe rag" as in "Write the bloody story, you bloody toe rag!"

The occupants of the *Post*'s table had a suitable attitude about the evening and proceeded to lampoon the show and everyone in it. Most of their remarks were unprintable. I ended up having a very good time, although it was quite a while before I was able to think about the Fred Richmond incident without cringing. Had I just been a guest, or was there really a hidden motive in the invitation? Politics certainly could be perplexing.

Although the power possessed by some politicians automatically renders them gossip column candidates, that doesn't mean all politicians are apt as story subjects. Like glamorous movie legends who turn out to be tacky and uncouth, or, even more unthinkable, human, politicians are often disappointing in person.

During presidential election years, candidates make the rounds of different cities, and during these trips drop by local newspapers for meetings with editorial boards. As the editor of Page Six, I would be asked to join some of these meetings—ostensibly to toss in a provocative question or two. During the two I sat in on in 1984, I didn't ask any questions. In serious need of a cattle prod to stay awake, I blinked violently and constantly to help maintain a vertical position.

Gary Hart was then well on the way to establishing a position that would make him the Democrats' frontrunner in 1988, before Donna Rice and the Monkey Business knocked him on his political posterior. Forced to recall, specifically, anything he said during his meeting with the *Post*'s editors, I would draw a complete blank, other than to say "issues." He talked a lot about issues. I yawned.

John Glenn was no more thrilling. Even the revved-up right-wingers from the *Post*'s editorial section couldn't ignite any fire in this guy.

It was sort of depressing. When you work for a newspaper, particularly on a newspaper's gossip column, you stop thinking of politicians as individuals for whom you might cast a vote. You think about them in terms of copy. You want them to be lively and quick. You want them to be scintillating, even shocking. You want them to be quotable, for heaven's sake.

During one display of publicly outrageous behavior by a politician, I got all excited, only to conclude I couldn't even write about it.

There I was at a restaurant on the Upper East Side with a friend who happened to be involved in Democratic politics when in strolled a well-known Democratic senator, sloshed to the gills and accompanied by a young woman who'd looked like she'd been sprung from boarding school for the evening. My eyes widened. They sat down to join us. The senator ordered more drinks, then he started talking about his future, which, in his estimation, was so bright as to be blinding.

The '84 presidential election was inconsequential, he said. The '88 race was all that mattered—and he'd be at the head of the Democratic pack. He practically had the nomination in the bag already, god damn it. Just take a look at the rest of the so-called candidates, and then cast an appraising eye on him, and his astounding credentials. It was only a matter of time before 1600 Pennsylvania Avenue would be his address.

Well, now, wasn't this special. Most of the time, when someone starts foaming at the mouth in front of me, unaware that I write a gossip column, I give them the benefit of the doubt and ignore the information, particularly if it's a casual situation in which I'm not really working.

But I had met this guy before, at a party in Washington. And I'd had lunch with him, and he knew I wrote for a newspaper, or at least he should have known.

Every time I started to say something, my friend interrupted, or kicked me under the table while giving me desperate looks. The senator kept talking. If I'd had a tape recorder, I would have had enough stuff to fill the column for days, even weeks.

Finally, a table at the other end of the restaurant emptied and the senator and his date moved. My friend was in a frenzy.

"You can't write any of that."

"Why not? He knows I write a column."

"He must have forgotten. This dinner was supposed to be off-the-record."

"As far as you're concerned, not him."

"You can't do it. He'll blame it on me. He was drunk. Haven't you ever been drunk?"

The guilt started to seep in. Haven't you ever done or said something you regretted? What if you'd done or said it in front of a gossip columnist? Would you want it written about? Now, isn't that a double standard? Would that be fair?

I didn't write anything, but not because I'd had a few too many myself once or twice. I justified my actions by the fact that my friend, a good source of information, threatened to stop speaking to me if I did.

The sloshed senator decided not to run for President in 1988, which was sort of too bad. He seemed no less suited for the job than most of the rest of the people going after it. And, if nothing else, he certainly would have been quotable.

When I first started writing about politics, my sources were mostly New York-based. I knew very few people involved in national politics, and relied on more experienced reporters, like the *Post*'s Deborah Orin, for advice on those kinds of stories.

On my first out-of-town assignment, I couldn't depend on another reporter to help me out. The person who saved my ass on that occasion was someone I'd previously detested, Roy Cohn.

When Cohn died, there was mourning among reporters, not so much for the loss of the man, but for the loss of a great news source. Cohn, infamous for his involvement in Senator Joseph McCarthy's Communist witch-hunting in the 1950s, was an incurable news junkie. A powerful political operative both locally and nationally, Cohn fed information to reporters at most, if not all, news organizations in New York.

Claudia Cohen knew Roy Cohn and, because the assistant picked up the phone at Page Six, I put his calls through to her. The first time it happened I expressed my disgust. "How can you talk to him?" I asked her. "After what he did with McCarthy?"

Claudia's response was: "Grow up."

I paid no attention and availed myself of every opportunity to express my distaste for Cohn and his politics.

Soon after Jim Brady took over Page Six, Ronald Reagan was elected for the first time, and the *Post* began preparing its inauguration coverage. Not much was done about selecting reporters to cover the social beat until a day or two before the inaugural festivities were to take place. Asked if he was interested in going to Washington, Brady declined. Jokingly, I suggested taking the assignment. "Good idea," said Brady.

With twenty-four hours left until the inaugural events were to begin, I was told to go home, pack and get to the airport. I had no credentials, no hotel room, no ball gown and minimal sources. "Don't worry," said editor Steve Dunleavy. "Call Roy. He'll take care of it."

And he did. He rounded up passes to two or three of the inaugural balls, and also invited me to a cocktail party he was throwing. Barbara Walters, Andy Warhol, Warren Avis, Estée Lauder, and disco owner Régine were among the presumably rabid Reaganites in attendance.

Cohn also came to my rescue when I tried to enter the first of the inaugural balls. Clad in a black jumpsuit that had on prior occasions fit the description "black tie," I was informed it didn't fit the Reagan definition of black tie: women were required to wear dresses. Though sporting a dread center-seamed garment, I felt right at home. At Catholic school, the rules had been the same.

Outside the entrance to the New York State ball, I ducked to the side of the security men to try and find Cohn, and in the process ran into Richard Johnson, then a reporter at the *Post*'s city desk. Wearing a dark suit instead of a tuxedo, he too was a wardrobe violator, another GOP fashion victim. We convinced another reporter to go in and track down Cohn for us. A few minutes later, he came bounding toward the entrance and pulled one of the security men aside. We were in.

As a final bit of media aid, Cohn leaked several stories to me, and introduced me to a couple of other news sources as well. Upon returning to New York, I received a note from Roger Wood congratulating me on the job I'd done. Somehow, it seemed Cohn was the one who deserved the note.

Cohn's cocktail party received substantial coverage in the *Post*. He obviously had reason to be helpful, and I didn't delude myself that he'd done so to prove he was really a nice guy. Cohn always had an agenda, but that didn't detract from the fact that he knew, or represented, an astounding number of powerful people in New York— real estate magnate Donald Trump and Yankees owner George Steinbrenner among them. He also maintained close ties to the Reagan White House.

Because Cohn was cooperative, I didn't balk at doing the occasional favor for him after I became the editor of Page Six, keeping up my end of a tacit, quid pro quo agreement. If he'd helped with a couple of political stories, and then called about some social event he was organizing, perhaps one of his birthday parties, which were always lavish and drew an eclectic group of guests, from fashion designers to judges, I'd run an item about the party. Why not? His drew as many big names as any other event we covered.

My contact with Cohn concerned material for the column, and took place primarily over the phone. I never came to know him well personally. He was friendly with other editors, however, including metropolitan editor Steve Dunleavy. Cohn's ties to the city desk eventually interfered with Page Six's coverage of him.

Not long before Cohn died, in August of 1986, he lost his license to practice law in New York State, disbarred by the Appellate Division of the state supreme court. The decision was reached after an investigation into four cases involving charges of misconduct on Cohn's part.

Cohn's supporters decried the action, saying it was an insensitive blow against an individual weakened by debilitating illness. Why now, they argued, when he's unable to fight back?

His disbarment was front-page news in New York. When I saw it on the front page of the *Post,* my jaw dropped, though at that point, the story was too big to ignore. The paper could have had a scoop on it more than three years earlier.

When the disciplinary committee of the Appellate Division began investigating Cohn's conduct early in 1983, I was tipped off to the story by our state supreme court reporter, Hal Davis. The most diligent of all Page Six's staff sources, Davis is the type of reporter who feels personal disappointment if what he views as a great story doesn't make it into the paper. He called us three or four times a week with interesting legal matters, of the sort that didn't really warrant a news story, but were perfect for Page Six.

He was very excited about the Cohn story. If the high-powered attorney were to be disbarred—and it looked like there was a good case—it would be a big news story; we could lay claim to having been onto it first. Though Cohn had been helpful to me, I didn't feel this granted him immunity from any but positive coverage on Page Six. I was certain he'd be pragmatic about it as well.

I called Cohn to inquire about the investigation. He must have contacted Dunleavy immediately, because, a few minutes after I'd spoken with Cohn, I was called to the city desk. Dunleavy asked what kind of nonsense I was trying to write about Cohn. It wasn't nonsense, I explained. An investigation into alleged misconduct by a major power broker was an excellent story.

Was I a mental defective, Dunleavy wanted to know? Cohn was one of the paper's most important sources, Dunleavy informed me. How could I even contemplate running such a negative story about one of our best news sources, especially a story without any merit?

It was my impression, I told Dunleavy, that the disciplinary committee would decide the merit of the charges against Cohn. Dunleavy said I should drop the story. If I pursued it, he told me, it would be killed from the column.

At first, I hesitated. It was a good story, and perhaps, if I wrote it and had the finished product for ammunition, I might be able to argue it into the paper. On the other hand, I'd faced this sort of ultimatum before. If I wrote the Cohn story, and left the office without resolving the issue, I likely would pick up the paper the next day and find the story had been killed. In its stead, I would see a story I had not written appear under my byline. I dropped the Cohn story.

Though Page Six functioned separately from the news desk, it couldn't escape some of the internal political decisions that affected all editorial departments. Like the shit list.

The shit list—containing the names of people who were

Not Our Friends—was subject to such frequent change that I several times put tongue in cheek and requested regularly revised copies of it in writing. No one laughed, nor did they make up a formal list.

It certainly would have made my life easier if Rupert Murdoch had put down on paper names not to be mentioned in the paper, but I was never certain how much input he had into the informal compendium. It may have been a case of others second-guessing him by assuming he wanted someone banned from the pages of the *Post*.

Conservative editor and writer William F. Buckley, Jr., whose syndicated column ran in the *Post*, hit the shit list when he defected to the *Daily News*. I was told that Buckley's name was not to be mentioned in the paper, and wasn't, intentionally, for quite some time. In a case of guilt by matrimonial association, the name of his wife, Pat Buckley, was also stricken from the *Post*'s record, which made life complicated for those covering society functions. The Buckleys are one of the most social couples in New York. They attend, and she sometimes organizes, many of New York's big galas. When one occurred, and the Buckleys were in attendance, they were not listed among the guests in the *Post*'s post-party coverage.

Occasionally, someone would forget, and Buckley's name would slip into a news story, or one of the other gossip columns. When that happened, I would charge into the city room, brandishing the paper: "Why are they allowed to mention him, and we're not?" Always, I was told, it was an error—and the guilty party would be properly chastised.

Television host and commentator David Frost was high on the shit list. Apparently, he'd had Murdoch as a guest on a London talk show several years earlier and had asked the press baron questions Murdoch had been assured would not be asked. That's the reason I was given, in any case, when I was told Frost was persona non grata.

For a time, "Saturday Night Live" was also banned from the paper, the result of its regular satirizations of the *Post.* One editor told me not to write about the show "unless they are canceled and we can say 'good riddance.' "

Paul Newman occupied the apex of the shit list. During the filming of *Fort Apache, the Bronx* in New York in 1980, a photo taken on the set of the movie appeared on Page Six, with this caption: "Paul Newman stares in astonishment as a 'Fort Apache' crew member wards off a group of Hispanic youths protesting the film." The story involved supposedly anti-*Fort Apache* groups criticizing the film's content.

An outraged Newman slammed the story as untrue and unfair, and, after that, never talked to the press without expressing his opinions of the *Post* and its owner.

In an interview with *Rolling Stone* in 1983, he said the film *Absence of Malice* was "a direct attack on the New York Post. Well, put it this way: I was emotionally receptive to doing a piece about sloppy journalism. I wish I could sue the Post, but it's awfully hard to sue a garbage can."

Newman told the magazine that he hated Rupert Murdoch almost as much as he hated nuclear warheads, and he wouldn't minding ridding the world of both menaces. He said he dreamed of getting even: "What someone might do is invent something. Something really insulting. Like Murdoch can't spell and has to carry a pocket dictionary. That he got picked up at a very early age for having sex with chickens."

No, Newman was not real popular at the *Post.* Nothing was to be written about him, I was informed, except, of course, if something really horrible happened, such as Newman driving a racing car off a cliff. On a couple of occasions, when I had a newsworthy story involving Newman, I asked that an exception be made, but to no avail. Newman was so loathed at the *Post* that for a time his name was stricken from the *Post*'s TV guide. If a Paul Newman movie had been scheduled for television broadcast, the *Post* would describe it without mentioning Newman: *Hud,* starring Patricia Neal and Melvyn Douglas, or *The Hustler,* starring Jackie Gleason.

The theory behind the shit list was: if people dumped on the *Post,* or made fun of us, or DEFECTED TO THE COMPETITION, why should we be nice and write about them, the swine?

Many supported the validity of such a theory, but I was concerned primarily with material for the column, and the shit list cut down on item nominees. Also, I was forever forgetting who was still on the list, and who had done penance and had been absolved.

After digging up some tasty morsel about Paul Newman —perhaps a monumental world exclusive about his line of popcorn or salad dressing—I'd turn it in late in the day with the rest of the column only to be told: "You dolt! He's on the bloody shit list!" And then I'd have to dredge up a last-minute replacement.

Murdoch himself was on the list of banned names. If he and his wife Anna attended an event in New York, they were not to be listed on Page Six or in any of the other columns. That ban seems to have been lifted, and recently I've noticed Murdoch mentioned by Suzy, who left the *Daily News* to become the *Post*'s society gossip columnist in

1985, but, for most of the time I worked on Page Six, I was told that the paper's owner didn't want his name tossed about in its gossip columns.

Really, can you blame him?

Chapter 5

DESPERATE SEARCH FOR SOURCES

Let me take this opportunity to clear up some gross misconceptions about the tools of the gossip trade.

You don't need funny hats.

You don't need a choice table at "21."

You don't need a dagger, or stiletto heels.

You don't need a ruthless sidekick.

You don't really even need a typewriter.

Though all of this stuff—especially the hats and the sidekick—would be worthy additions to a gossip columnist's collection of professional instruments, they're superfluous. Forced to write a column from a desert island, the columnist would need only one tool—a bank of sources, plus, of course, a way to reach them.

Sources can be kept current in that imposing wheel of fortune, the Rolodex, or in a discreet leatherbound book. If the columnist has a good memory, baggage of any kind can be eliminated.

When Jim Brady quit the *Post* in 1983, I was named the editor of Page Six. Finally, officially, a gossip columnist, I waited for the overnight transformation.

I'm still waiting.

At the *Post*, short on material for the column, I continued to steer toward metropolitan editor Steve Dunleavy for assistance. He still said, "Grovel, bitch." When short on cash, I still went to city desk assistant Myron Rushetzky for a loan. He still shouted out, "Where the hell's my money?" when I walked through the city room. My promotion did not prompt Rupert Murdoch to drop by our office to seek my august editorial advice on matters of global importance.

There were no hats—not even a new pen and pencil set. And, most discouraging of all, I did not wake up one morning with hundreds of newly reliable sources rushing to be the first to call me with world exclusives.

Acquiring the title of editor did make certain immediate changes in my lifestyle, however. Wary of not finding enough material to fill the column, I started arriving at the office every morning at around eight-thirty, which was too early, really. Few of the people I needed to talk to about stories were in their offices at that hour. Few picked up their phones, in any case. But I never knew when a source might pop up with a hot item, and, as my supply of sources was still somewhat limited, I didn't want to risk losing an important story. Suppose a Priscilla Presley exclusive slipped through my fingers because I hadn't been there to take that all-important call? I shuddered to think.

Starting work early made going out at night complicated, but hitting the circuit was mandatory to picking up stories, and drumming up sources. Still, I wasn't certain how I'd be able to finish the column, go out to parties, get up in time to swim a few laps—something I tried to do every day to keep from becoming a degenerate—and be at my desk before nine, fueled and fortified for the gossip battle ahead.

One of the first events I attended in my new role as Page Six editor was a cocktail party at the home of writer Gay Talese. I didn't know very many people there, but Talese attempted to introduce me to a few. A writer I'd met several times before came up to congratulate me, commenting, "Now you have power, my dear."

If that was how he measured power, he was misinformed. I'd had almost as much impact on the column's content before, but with the circles of people in New York who really care about being written about in columns like Page Six, appearances are everything.

In the minds of people like him, I suddenly counted as something because my surface had improved. I'd not been worthy of serious consideration as an understudy, but now that I'd been fingered to take over the leading role on Page Six, a different stage had been set. He was all smarmy smiles.

Who's to say my opinion, in choosing, or not choosing, to write about someone, was more valid than anyone else's? It all seemed fairly phony to me, but, by working on the column, I was, in a sense, buying into this point of view, the one that measures value in superficial terms.

There were those who felt my surface needed work.

A public relations executive I'd encountered while Brady was editing Page Six asked me out to lunch not long after I took over the job. He seemed to be plugged into a variety of people and might prove a useful contact, so I said yes. During the meal, after informing me that "good-looking dames are at a premium in this town," he offered a few hints on how to succeed as a columnist. For one thing, he said, "Get rid of the *shmatte.*" I looked down at the dress I was wearing. It was from Saks—and it hadn't been on sale, either. Then, he advised, "you gotta start wearing makeup."

Okay, so the dress wasn't state-of-the-art equipment, but at least it fit. Where was I supposed to find the time to go shopping for new clothes? Or the hours needed to apply prodigious quantities of makeup? Seriously speaking, would the content of Page Six be affected by heavy applications of mascara?

At that point, all I cared about was getting the column written. When Brady left, so too departed the buffer between me and the other editors of the *Post.* Fearful that I wouldn't be able to handle the new responsibilities, my superiors made several trips per day into our office to check up on my progress.

I worked on presentation, learning to promote each piece as the most scintillating information to appear in a newspaper since the Pentagon Papers: "We have got the FUNNIEST story! It is REALLY a great item!" If I were to have said simply: "We've got a couple of interesting stories," each editor would have panicked, and doubled or tripled his visits.

When not previewing coming attractions, I was occupied with comments on past feature presentations.

Before taking over Page Six, I'd fielded my share of complaints about gossip items, but the majority were handled by the editor of the column. Until assuming the post myself, I hadn't been fully aware of how often people called to raise a fuss. We carefully checked information, but it was still disconcerting to pick up the phone and hear an outraged voice declare a story to be total fabrication.

About a month after starting the new job, I received a phone call at home on a Saturday morning from the editor of a small drama publication in New York who accused us of stealing a story from him. He said he'd been duped and ripped off, he had all his phone conversations with members of the Page Six staff on tape and he was going to sue. I looked into the matter on Monday morning and discovered no grounds for his accusations, but he'd still managed to ruin my weekend.

The same week, a representative for Lauren Bacall called to complain about two Page Six stories on Bacall, one involving Yoko Ono's bodyguards. Bacall and Ono lived in the same apartment building, and we'd reported that Bacall had protested to the management about the bodyguards running around with their guns prominently displayed. Bacall's representative said it wasn't true. Again, I went back over the details. No matter how confident I was about a story, yells, screams and threats threw me off guard and I would go over all the ground already covered to reassure myself that we had been right in what we'd written.

Complaints came not only from residents of New York. Several weeks after an item on Atlanta's Mayor Andrew Young appeared, he called the *Post*. According to the Page Six story, Young had jumped into an occupied cab in midtown Manhattan, and practically hijacked it to the airport. Young said the item had been incorrect, perhaps a case of mistaken identity. "On at least one occasion," Young explained, "people have said to me, 'Mr. Bond, may I have your autograph?' And I just sign Julian Bond."

For the most part, complaints are unwarranted and come from people disgruntled that a story has appeared in print. If the facts are right, they can complain as loud and as long as they please and they won't see any sort of correction. If the subject of a story proves information is incorrect, however, a retraction or correction appears.

Upon occasion, complaints result not necessarily in corrections, but in even more newsworthy follow-up stories.

When a reliable Page Six source called with a story about John Kennedy, Jr., renting an X-rated movie at a video store—then failing to return it—facts were checked. Staffers at the Upper East Side video store said the son of the late JFK had come in with his girlfriend and picked up a couple of movies—Woody Allen's *Broadway Danny Rose* and a steamy feature called *Bodacious Ta-Ta's.* The store's video catalogue summarized the plot of the latter as involving "four frisky, well-endowed strippers who'll do anything for a good time."

The real meat of the story was the fact that John, Jr., had failed to return the videos he'd rented using an American Express card. Calls to Kennedy weren't returned.

The day the story ran, Kennedy called Page Six himself, claiming he was the victim of mistaken identity, as far as the renting of *Bodacious Ta-Ta's* was concerned. We ran a follow-up with his comments. "It's a complete lie," he said. "If I were going to rent an adult film, I would never use my American Express card. How stupid can someone be?"

Kennedy admitted that he'd neglected to return *Broadway Danny Rose,* however, and thanked us for reminding him. "I'd completely forgotten about it," he said.

Prior to my taking over Page Six, and after, we'd written about a divorce action involving Count Enrico Carimati and his wife Cristina, then the owners of a chic jewelry store on Madison Ave. The primary source of the stories had been a reporter at the *Post*'s city desk. Unhappy with Page Six's coverage, Carimati, whose attorney was

Roy Cohn, had his public relations person, Pamela Murdock, call me to arrange a lunch to discuss the matter. She scheduled it at Le Cirque, the restaurant popular with New York's most visible society mavens, the regular midday trough for the "Ladies Who Lunch." I'd never been there before and was interested in checking out the scene, and the food, reputed to be superior to the *Post*'s cafeteria.

Murdock and I arrived at the same time; Carimati was nearly an hour late. While we were waiting, I began to realize that the lunch might not have been such a hot idea. Not only was Carimati unhappy with the manner in which his divorce was being covered, Murdock told me, he was livid.

Carimati finally arrived, and turned on the Mediterranean charm for about five minutes. Then he cut the crap and got down to business. He said a reporter from the *Post* —as it turned out, the reporter who'd tipped me off to several of the Carimati stories—had been having an affair with his estranged wife.

"He has been naked in my apartment," he declared of the reporter. Aware of the looks we were getting from adjoining tables as the level of his voice began to rise, along with the intensity of his hand gestures, I looked down at the menu. It wasn't as appealing as it had appeared moments earlier.

I told him I knew nothing about naked reporters in his apartment, and was only aware of the facts as we had reported them. We'd gotten his side of things, I said, from his attorney, Roy Cohn. (I didn't know what to call the guy, either. He had a lot of names. Count? Kiko? Ricky? Mr. Carimati?) Carimati said Cohn was unfamiliar with some details of his case, including rent payments on the apartment where his estranged spouse was living with their son. "I'm Italian," he said. "Roy tells me to pay nothing. The court now says I have to pay nothing. But am I going to leave my son without a place to live? No. Her, my wife, I don't care. It's only my son I care about."

Carimati explained his tardiness: "Do you know why I am late? I go to Cerutti to buy my son underwear. His mother, she doesn't buy him underwear, and the New York *Post* says she is such a good mother." I couldn't imagine what underwear might cost at Cerutti, the pricey European children's store. More than Carter spankies, I bet.

At this point, my lunch sat before me cold and untouched. My appetite had waned as Carimati's gesticulations had waxed expressive—and everyone in the restaurant was staring at us. He said he would sue if we ever wrote about him again.

Back at the office, I went over the stories about the divorce, which reassured me that we'd gotten comments from Carimati's side. I approached the reporter who'd been the source of some of the stories. He denied Carimati's accusations. I had no reason not to believe him. He'd proven a reliable source of information on many other occasions.

There are very few sources, regardless of whether they are feeding information to a city desk or a gossip column, who don't have a hidden agenda, or an ax to grind. If Carimati had been right, and this reporter had been having an affair with his wife, I wouldn't have been real thrilled about it, but I had no evidence. What I had were the reporter's denial and the stories about the divorce, which were accurate and which presented both sides of the case.

I called Roy Cohn to inquire further about his client's complaints. Cohn said he thought the Page Six stories had been fair. "Besides," Cohn noted pragmatically, "the entire world is not waiting with bated breath for news of the Carimatis. He should be glad he got mentioned. He should start to worry when people stop paying attention." I reminded myself never to hire Cohn if I found myself in legal trouble.

I didn't write much about the Carimatis after that. I also began to place more regular calls to the attorneys at Squadron, Ellenoff, Plesent and Lehrer, the firm representing both Rupert Murdoch and the *Post*. Whenever a story looked sensitive—or if it involved a legal matter in which a nuance in language or tone might prove important—I called one of our lawyers and had it "legaled."

Quickly, I learned there is no such thing as a surplus of sources. In certain areas, I was covered and always had someone to call when I needed information. In others, my contacts were woefully inadequate.

Upon meeting someone in a field where I was poorly connected, I'd have to suppress the urge to pounce on him or her—"Okay, you're my new source"—and go about the coddling and wooing in a leisurely fashion, taking the person out to lunch or dinner, and not imposing too quickly, or else the spigots of information would turn off before they'd even begun to flow.

As I began to dip my toes into Manhattan's social waters, I met more and more people in different fields, some of whom I stayed in touch with as sources. The column brought in many of its own sources, too, without much effort on my part. With those, I didn't even have to leave the office.

Regular calls and letters seeped in from "the Mole," a *Wall Street Journal* staffer who never missed an opportunity to pass along information regarding the operation of the paper and its parent company, Dow Jones. Staff disputes, interoffice memos—he told us everything, effusive in his delight at leaking stories. One letter, which began with news that a previous story on Page Six had "got 'em at each other's throats in the executive suite," ended with "I've got to quit now because I don't want to get too/close to you, darleeng. We might even begin trading gossip, and we certainly don't wish to do that. Just when are we going to have lunch and whatever, darling woman??? The Dreaded Mole."

Some of the Mole's stories were a bit too inside for Page Six, but many were of general interest and I used them. Because I had no idea who he was, all of the tips emanating from Mr. Mole, which was how he identified himself on the phone, had to be scrutinized more carefully than usual. I don't recall him ever being wrong on one, though.

Another source was a writer I'll refer to here as "the Tattler." An uncontrollable gossip, the Tattler would call Page Six from phone booths in restaurants, from quiet corners during dinner parties in private homes, from his agent's office the moment his agent stepped out—anywhere he picked up what he referred to as "good dish." Though I knew who he was and had had dinner with him several times, I still felt the Tattler had to be checked out extra carefully—if only because I was wary of how eager he was to plant information.

The Tattler told me that he saw a psychiatrist five times a week, and that most of the sessions dealt with his irrepressible urge to gossip. I felt a little guilty, imagining that his weekly shrink bill had to be pretty hefty. Perhaps I should refuse to use his information. If his outlet were to be closed, maybe he'd be able to deal with his problem.

There didn't seem much point in that. He'd just find another outlet. He already had more than one.

After I'd passed on a story he'd given me, I saw it in another column. It wasn't unusual to see a story a press agent had attempted to plant turn up elsewhere, but the Tattler was not a press agent. I knew the story had to have come from him because the minute details were identical to those he'd given me. The next time he called, I mentioned it to him. "Oh, I call her too," he said of the other columnist, adding, "But I call you first." My response was: "I bet you say that to all the columnists."

Of the sources I've learned to trust, most don't have personal stakes in the information they impart. Even with longtime, trusted sources, however, there are often hidden agendas. Why, after all, do most people become sources if not to further their own interests, or to knock down those of an enemy?

With some sources, I can't figure it out. Of my dozen best sources, half have little or nothing to gain from giving me information. Are they simply nice, helpful people? In the dog-eat-dog world of the media, the notion is farfetched, but it seems to have a basis in fact. One of my best sources works for another news organization in New York. He's been giving me great stories for years and has never asked me for a favor, never said, "Do you think you could run an item on . . ."

The most questionable sources of information are anonymous letters or phone calls. If sources won't identify themselves, you can bet they've got an agenda, and it's rarely hidden.

My rule on checking out unidentified dirt dishers is: one phone call. The tipster might be a raving lunatic, and prolonged investigation into the information may prove fruitless, not to mention embarrassing, for the person doing the investigating. Still, it's worth a phone call.

There are other sorts of tips, some anonymous, some from people I know, that fall into the category of sheer, salacious rumor. In this category, I have heard everything. So-and-so is bisexual. So-and-so is cheating on his wife. So-and-so is having an affair with an orangutan. As far as most newspapers are concerned, this is not material fit to print, even if true.

Once a rumor gets going in New York, a startling number of people, many of them in the media, pass it along. One theory maintains that reporters and editors are frustrated by the amount of unprintable information they come across, and must spread it orally to relieve the urge to communicate. I certainly can't say I always have been sensible in this department, having made my share of phone calls beginning with the words "You're not going to believe what I heard," but I've become more careful after observing the damage potential in an unfounded rumor.

In recent years, the most malicious rumors have involved AIDS. Every time a celebrity looks ill, the rumor mill starts churning with the story that AIDS has struck once again.

The first of these rumor campaigns—and the most elaborate—involved designer Calvin Klein. I didn't pay much attention to the first few anonymous calls, but once they'd escalated to three or four a week, and some came from people I knew, they were hard to ignore. One caller said his brother was a doctor at St. Luke's, where Klein had been admitted. Another said her sister was an X-ray technician at Mount Sinai, where Klein also was supposed to be a patient. The calls became very detailed, from people purporting to work, or have friends or relatives who

97

worked, at virtually ever hospital in New York—all of them claiming Klein had been admitted with AIDS-related symptoms.

Other New York columnists, including Liz Smith, were getting the same calls. A radio station on the West Coast aired a story saying Klein had died. The rumor spread to such an extent that in 1983 Klein was compelled to talk to the press, to deny he was suffering from any life-threatening disease. He also began to show up at more public events. Not long after the rumors started, I saw him at the Tony Awards in New York, with Bianca Jagger on his arm, and looking not at all like someone on the verge of death.

Some time later, the same rumors started about another designer, Perry Ellis. I had found no fact in the Klein rumors, and didn't print them. The circumstances surrounding the rumors of Ellis having AIDS were similar. Several months after the Ellis rumors started, however, the designer died, reportedly of an AIDS-related illness.

In the final analysis, a columnist is only as good as his or her sources. Building up a bank of reliable ones from which to draw information is a painstakingly tedious process, sort of like constructing your own skyscraper, by hand.

A friend fascinated by gossip quizzed me about the job: "Do you actually know all these people? Do you know Michael Jackson?"

I looked at him like he'd gone off the deep end. Of course I don't know Michael Jackson. Not well, anyway. A columnist often has contact with the celebrity subjects of the column's stories, but developing friendships with celebrities is not the best mode of operation. The columnist is supposed to be covering these people, not becoming best buddies with them.

If Michael Jackson were my best friend—a very remote possibility, since he prefers the company of children, pets and skeletons over adults, particularly press adults—I'd feel obligated to check in with him whenever I wrote about him. Also, it's been my experience, with celebrities I do know well enough to call personally, that they will want to rewrite the story in their own fashion, or attempt to kill it:

"Don't say the producer fired me. Say I had a better offer from a better studio. And while you're at it, throw in that the producer is a pimp and a drug dealer, and he wears women's underwear."

An actor I became friendly with was for a time the focus of numerous gossip column items. After I got to know him, I felt I should call him whenever I came across newsworthy information involving him, for a comment or a quote. His response was always the same: "You don't want to print that. I mean, who cares?"

If I made a case for running the story, by saying that the information would get out eventually—so why not have it be through me?—he would counter with "I'm not ready to talk about it. I promise I'll call you as soon as the story is ready to break. C'mon, you're a friend, do me this one favor."

Ninety percent of the time, when I try to be nice and hold a story until someone is ready to release it, I lose it to another columnist. In the gossip business, niceness, and a token, will get you a ride on the subway. Still, it pays to be nice sometimes, lest you die and wind up in gossip columnist hell—a disco filled with press agents reciting lines from *Moose Murders.*

In March of 1983, between Claus von Bülow's two trials on charges he attempted to murder his wife Sunny, I got a call from a woman named Andrea Reynolds. From what I knew at that point, Andrea's husband, producer Sheldon Reynolds, was a friend of Von Bülow's and had been acting as his press spokesman. He'd also been functioning as Von Bülow's agent in the sale of a book on the Danish socialite's experiences. I wasn't certain where Andrea Reynolds fit in.

I met the couple for lunch at Mortimer's, another eatery favored by the social set. This time, no one screamed at me about naked reporters. Both Andrea and Sheldon Reynolds wanted to discuss the second Von Bülow trial, during which he'd appeal his conviction in the first. They were extremely well versed in the legal particulars, particularly Andrea, who rattled off specifics from affidavits. I was curious about their involvement, but they said they were simply friends of Von Bülow's who'd become outraged at what they viewed as an injustice and who wanted to do what they could to right an alleged wrong.

Von Bülow wasn't speaking to the press at that point, and I figured it might not be a bad idea to get on good terms with the couple. Perhaps, when the time came for Von Bülow to talk, he might talk to the *Post*.

Andrea, a stylishly vivacious Hungarian whose conversation was punctuated with numerous "Daalings" (at this point, I'd come to the conclusion that I was the only one in New York who didn't start conversations with "Daaling"!), obviously hoped to establish a friendly relationship with Page Six to attempt to get us to write about Von Bülow's trials and tribulations from his point of view.

For a time, I laid off Von Bülow, in the hopes that I might get the first interview with him. I didn't. Andrea, who eventually left her husband and moved in with Von Bülow, continued to push for the airing of the Von Bülow grievances. She sometimes called me at home, always stressing that we were "friends" and I was "a trustworthy journalist."

She was a useful contact, but I had no interest in becoming great friends with Andrea and Von Bülow. I was interested in material for Page Six. They were a flamboyant pair and made entertaining copy. Between the two trials, it was peculiarly fascinating to watch Von Bülow and Andrea rise to the top of New York society, becoming much-sought-after guests at the chicest parties. Strangely enough, their stars seemed to fade after the second trial, when Von Bülow was cleared of any criminal wrongdoing.

They invited me to a couple of cocktail parties at their Fifth Avenue apartment, the one Von Bülow had shared with his wife Sunny until she fell into her likely irreversible coma.

The first time I boarded the elevator in their building, I expected it to open as most elevators do, into a hall of doors leading to different apartments. This one led directly into their spacious and sumptuously appointed quarters. Some of the guests were names recognizable from regular appearances in society columns. There was much bussing of the air next to ears and exclamations of "Daaling, so good to see you! It's been ages!" Only at this party, the host had been convicted of attempting to murder his wife by injecting her with insulin.

The conviction hadn't put a damper on the Von Bülow wit.

Von Bülow, whose bearing was regal, never talked about himself. A conversation with him consisted primarily of anecdotes. He'd tell an amusing tale about his days in London working for J. Paul Getty or of an encounter with some behemoth of European society. The anecdotes were always well delivered, with precisely aimed punchlines.

I once went out to lunch with Andrea and Von Bülow, to an Italian restaurant on the East Side. I'd had to cancel a previous lunch due to illness. They asked about my health. I said I had been very rundown but, after a series of B_{12} injections, was feeling better.

"Daaling," said Andrea. "You must give me the name of your doctor. Vitamin injections are so wonderful, but it is so difficult to find American doctors who will give them. They are so ridiculous about injections in this country."

"Now, now, girls," chuckled Von Bülow. "You know how I am about injections."

When Andrea did not like a story that had appeared on Page Six about Von Bülow, she would call to complain about its "slant." One night, I returned to my apartment to find a message from her on my answering machine about a story she hadn't liked: "Daaling," she said, "I thought we were friends."

A friendly relationship with celebrities proves positive if those celebrities come to me first to leak information, or grant difficult-to-obtain access, but more often than not the information they are willing to leak is of a highly positive nature. If an actor is thrown off the set of a movie for slugging the director, he's not likely to call me about it.

Building sources is a catch-22 process. To infiltrate the worlds covered in a gossip column, the columnist has to establish friendly relationships with a certain number of the column's subjects, but there is a line across which it is dangerous to tread.

Getting to know someone too well is a built-in obsolescence factor for a gossip columnist, or any journalist for that matter. I rarely write about the people I know the best.

Right after Jim Brady left Page Six, I got a tip about something that had happened at Mortimer's. While exiting the restaurant, designer Bill Blass had toppled a table full of drinks all over two women diners, without stopping to apologize. Said one witness: "He never even said, 'Can I replace the drink you're wearing?' It was amazing." At first, the owner of Mortimer's said he doubted such a thing had happened, then called back and admitted it had —but said Blass had been "extremely gracious" about the whole thing. Blass wouldn't talk to me, but an assistant to the designer said: "Mr. Blass knows nothing about this incident and whatever it was, it was highly exaggerated."

Brady called to see how I was doing with the column. I told him the Blass story.

"I don't know that I'd have run that," he said.

"Why not?" I asked.

"Blass is a good source," he explained, "not to mention a friend."

Well, he wasn't a friend of mine, and I ran the story. I thought Brady was being overly sensitive. The incident had happened. We had all sorts of witnesses and quotes. What difference would it have made if he had run the story while he had been editor?

A lot. I've run into a number of difficulties of my own in this area. If a story involving a friend passes my way, sometimes I'll run it. At other times, I'll label myself too close to the situation and drop the item.

Using close friends and family as sources is the most troublesome. If someone is known to be a good friend of mine, he or she might be pegged as a source, rendering it too problematic to use that person as such.

Some people are slightly paranoid about becoming sources. A good friend from college who's never given me a story, or even an idea for one, assumes I'm always working.

She regularly prefaces statements with, "This is off-the-record, you know," and then proceeds to tell me something that has happened to her while shopping, or in her aerobics class.

If a friend is willing to help out in the never-ending quest for items, it's fine by me, but I never push anyone who isn't interested. If everything said during a casual dinner conversation were potential material for the column, I'd eat alone every night.

Also, there is a knack to spotting what makes an item, a knack not indigenous to many of my friends, who seem to suffer from the "If I know about it, it must not be news" syndrome.

Most of the members of my family suffer from the syndrome as well, with one exception.

On the first day of Harvard's 350th anniversary celebration, I sat at my desk wondering if that day's pile of press releases would yield an honest-to-God, bona fide item, or yet another paper cut. The phone rang.

"Don't you dare put me on hold. We're at Harvard Yard, and I've got an item. Prince Charles was stung by a bee."

"Mom, you intrepid stringer, you. Are you having a good time?"

"Yes, but your father is getting very impatient. I had to wait a long time for the phone. Can you use the story?"

"Sounds promising. Any details on the injury?"

"It's only a bee sting, for heaven's sake. I've got the *Crimson*. There might be something in that. Let me look through it and I'll call you back."

Sometimes my mother's items are of dubious origin, but at least she tries.

"Do you want a Teddy Pendergrass item? He sang at a benefit downtown."

"Did you go?"

"Well, no. Actually, I got it out of the Philadelphia *Inquirer.*"

"But, Mom, I'm syndicated in the *Inquirer.* Suppose I steal it from them, and then it goes right back on the syndication wire?"

"Who's going to notice? Nobody has read about it in New York, have they?"

She had a point. I used the story. My mother is also very helpful with advance information on Broadway shows, which often hit Philadelphia en route to New York.

"Theresa and Winnie and I went to see *Sophisticated Ladies.* I think you should do an item about it."

"So, what's the item? Did anything happen?"

"No, but we liked it. You could say the tap dancing was very good."

With sources I don't know well, I ask myself a lot of questions.

Can I trust this person? Why is he leaking me information? What does she have up her sleeve? Is his partner lying? Do I call the lawyers?

During the time I wrote Page Six, I had dreams about items, dreams that became nightmares when there weren't enough to fill the column. In one recurring dream, I would open the paper looking for Page Six and wouldn't find it. Page five would be followed by page seven, skipping the column, which, apparently, I'd been unable to complete the day before.

In some of the dreams, I'd have enough stories to fill the space, but they'd be all wrong and everyone would call to complain, and threaten law suits.

No matter how productive a day had been, there would rarely be any material left over for the next Page Six. Along with the nine to twelve items needed for the column, a couple of extra stories, referred to as overmatter, were also required, in case of a problem or emergency leading to the spiking of a story after I'd left the office.

Filling a column is like placing a large sum of money in an empty bank vault, then immediately drawing out portions to pay bills: one moment, you are confident of a supportive cushion of cash; the next, all the money is gone, even the pocket change, and the following day you are back at the beginning, broke.

Effort is wasted in attempting to store items away for a slow day. The material is supposed to be timely, and "timeless" items quickly become dated, or appear somewhere else, rendering them useless to columns trading in "exclusive" material. Once one column has printed a story, it is knocked from the purview of a rival.

In the early part of my Page Six tenure, I began to understand why many newspaper people drink. After building into the fever pitch of deadline hour, I often would finish the column and leave the office with one thing in mind—a drink, or several drinks. If I happened to be out attending some column-related function on one of those nights, the hours were ill-spent. The next morning, the details of the stories I'd collected would be fuzzy, at best.

On those days, I would pray for quiet, for a silent, reliable influx of information that would be simple to confirm, and even simpler to write.

There are certain sources that never stop flowing. These steady streams are known as press agents.

To borrow from St. Terese and Truman Capote: "More tears are shed over answered prayers than unanswered ones."

Chapter 6

DEADLY FLACK ATTACK

There's a scene in *The Sweet Smell of Success*, in which Tony Curtis, as sleazy press agent Sidney Falco, is pleading with Burt Lancaster, who plays Walter Winchell-like gossip columnist J. J. Hunsecker, to run an item about one of his clients. Falco isn't successful.

Says J.J.: "You're dead. Go get yourself buried."

I saw the movie for the first time when Jim Brady was the editor of Page Six, and he took the staff on a field trip to the Regency, then a revival house on the Upper West Side, for a screening of the 1957 classic.

For months afterward, we quoted the movie and gave press agents J.J.-like turndowns: "Sidney, you're out of the column." Only the old-timers got the joke.

Before working on Page Six, I had no idea what a press agent was, but once I started in the newspaper business, the breed became a part of my daily existence. Everybody seemed to have a press agent, from the President of the United States (his is called the White House press secretary) to the owner of the Carnegie Deli.

Press agents are the only sources of information to which I've never had to feel beholden. They are paid to plant stories, to aid in the construction of a media image for their clients.

Sometimes I envision the world of celebrity journalism as a series of eggs. Inside each shell lurks a celebrity, with the most sought-after hiding behind hard-boiled exteriors guarded by battalions of press agents, or flacks, a term frequently used to described them. To get a crack at the celebrity's shell, a gossip columnist has to enlist the aid of the flacks, or work around them. There are also personalities whose shells long ago were broken and the contents scrambled who will try to serve journalists unsolicited omelets of information. For this, press agents also are hired. The tactics of certain press agents are worthy of observation.

It's unusual for me to hear directly from a celebrity seeking publicity. Publicity hounds call themselves, but the types of celebrities worth writing about shield themselves with press agents. There are press agents of numerous and varying breeds, all with distinctly personal styles of press relations.

Corporations, from banks to movie studios to manufacturers of auto parts, all have press agents, referred to as "corporate spokespersons." A corporate spokesperson has many duties, but, as far as a gossip columnist is concerned, their primary function is to field calls executives don't want to take. A call to an executive at Drexel Burnham Lambert regarding the rumored indictment of said executive is likely to be bounced to the corporate spokesperson's office. The spokesperson will go to the executive in question—the only one really qualified to answer the press queries—and deliberate about what to tell the columnist. In most cases, they will decide to say nothing, the old "no comment."

Though the columnist knows what will happen when a call is placed to a corporate executive, the call has to be made anyway. It's standard procedure. Also, you never know, the executive might pick up the phone accidentally and say something interesting. Not likely, but worth a try. There's also a chance the spokesperson might be a helpful one, willing to let loose with a piece of useful information.

Corporate spokespersons also try to promote events the corporation is sponsoring, and will send columnists and other press people releases heralding these events, often charity dinners, sometimes art exhibitions. When this happens, the columnist may remind the spokesperson that he or she was not too helpful the last time the columnist called about a news story. The spokesperson will then sigh and say, "Just doing my job."

There are also companies that specialize in public relations, many of them exclusively handling corporate p.r. work. A corporation eager to cover all bases will have a corporate spokesperson and an outside p.r. agency. This means the columnist has to make two phone calls for a "no comment."

Some of these outside agencies—Rogers & Cowan, Solters/Roskin/Friedman and P M K come readily to mind—handle mostly show business clients. The client may be a movie star, or a movie director. It may also be the movie itself. The show biz agencies are more helpful in confirming information about their clients, but a columnist has to be careful.

Certain press agents have relationships with other gossip columnists. If Columnist A calls to confirm that Movie Star B will be starring in Movie Director C's next movie, the press agent may confirm the information—but may also call Columnist B with the news, thereby depriving Columnist A of a full-blown scoop. It's difficult to prove that this has happened, but the number of alarming coincidences forces a columnist to take extra precautions. Safeguards include placing calls for confirmation so late in the day that the press agent won't have time to leak the story to a rival.

The show business press agents not only regulate access to a celebrity, they also control press events. Sometimes, the press agents will have to coerce journalists to attend, but frequently these events—movie screenings, Broadway openings and the like—are booked. In those cases, press agents have journalists coming to them seeking special dispensation.

Spokesperson, public relations person, publicist, press agent, flack, mouthpiece. The labels are different, but the functions are the same: shielding the client from direct dealings with an overly inquisitive press, and getting the client into the papers and on TV when the client wants to be there.

Public relations is a very big business. Many of the people involved in it are competent professionals whose duties are akin to those of advertising or marketing executives. The competent professionals do their share of dealing with gossip columns, but column planting isn't their main occupation.

The professional column planters are among the most persistent of the press agents. They're also, often unwittingly, the most entertaining.

For many of these flacks, time is suspended in the era of Walter Winchell and Leonard Lyons. Times have changed, but, thankfully, their styles haven't.

My favorite of all the old-time press agents was Sam Gutwirth, now retired, who represented mostly delis in New York, and who was shameless in hustling up an angle to get his clients a "column mention."

Gutwirth, who often worked from his home in Brooklyn, called everyone "doll." There were always a few phrases like "Watta ya say, doll, a column mention?" tossed into our conversations.

One conversation with Gutwirth went like this:

"Listen, doll, I think I gotta little item for you."

"What have you got?"

"Over at Star's Deli, on account of it's Greta Garbo's birthday, we gotta bust of her, in chopped liver."

"Very tasteful, Sam."

"Heh, heh. I knew you'd like that. That's not all, either. Also, on account of Greta's birthday and her being a senior, we're gonna give a free bowl of chicken soup to all seniors. You think you can use it?"

Sam Gutwirth items were classics, but there were only so many you could use in a given time period. At one point, having scored with an item involving heart-shaped matzoh balls in the chicken soup at Star's Deli on Valentine's Day, Gutwirth called Page Six before every conceivable holiday to report that Star's had come up with special matzoh balls to commemorate the occasion—St. Patrick's Day, the first day of spring, Flag Day, Paul McCartney's birthday. We ran a few of the items, but had to put the brakes on the matzoh ball express when one editor at the *Post* commented that we were overdoing it. "What next?" he asked. "Swastika-shaped matzoh balls for Hitler's birthday?"

Gutwirth usually phoned in his material, and only infrequently sent out press releases. When he did, they were worth saving. I hung on to one with three items, each plugging a different deli.

Tip Sheet

Event: The 30th anniversary of the opening of Dis-
         neyland will be commemorated with a
         chopped liver sculpture of Mickey Mouse, cre-
         ated by the Disney of chopped liver, Leo
         Steiner.
Where: Carnegie Deli . . . 854 7th Ave.
When: Wednesday . . . July 17th . . . TIME: 2 P.M.

Tip Sheet

Event: Red Skelton's 72nd birthday will be celebrated
         with free carrot cake to all coffee drinkers.
Where: Showtime Deli . . . 930 2nd Ave.
When: Thursday . . . July 18th . . . TIME: 1 P.M.

Tip Sheet

Event: The 16th anniversary of Armstrong and Al-
         drin's moon walk will be marked with free
         moon-shaped matzoh balls served in moon-
         colored chicken soup.
Where: Star's Deli . . . 593 Lex. Ave.
When: Saturday . . . July 20th . . . TIME: 1:30 P.M.

I have a hard time resisting items like these, or any of
the items from the old-time flacks, most of whom repre-
sent restaurants, clubs or Borscht Belt resorts and/or
Borscht Belt comedians. Saul Richfield, another of the
old-timers, once sent me a release declaring, "NATION'S
MOST BEAUTIFUL ATHLETES WILL DEVOUR STACKS OF SCHNITZEL IN
EATING CONTEST TO COMMEMORATE 200TH anniversary of ameri-
can-austrian relations."

113

Contained within the release was further information that "Six girls—foxy boxers, oil wrestlers, stunt women, Tai Chi expert, others—will be seated before platters stacked high with 15 different varieties of Schnitzel, including pizza schnitzel . . . Winner will receive $100 cash, several jogging outfits, other prizes and a roll of Tums."

Another classic came from a flack named Bob Nicolaides: "DREAMS, A GREENPOINT NITERY, FEATURES DEAF-MUTE SENIOR CITIZEN IN ITS LINE-UP OF MALE DANCERS." The release advised: "If you haven't seen yet a senior citizen strip down to his shorts and start doing the disco, hurry on down to Dreams," where the dancing senior citizen was "also a deaf-mute, which compounds the problem of communication, rendering it an amazing feat the fact that the dancer can follow the beat, when he cannot hear a sound."

When not dreaming up publicity stunts to promote their restaurants, the old-time flacks phone in the names of celebrities who've dined there. Because there are thousands of celebrities in the Naked City, all of whom eat out every night, I tell press agents I'm not interested in items declaring "Gene Kelly ate pizza at Ray's Famous." I need an angle.

If Robert Redford arrives at a restaurant and informs the waiter he is on a special diet allowing him to eat only skewered squid covered with caramel sauce, I'd call that an item. Or if he skewers his dining companion, that too would be worthy of note in a "column mention." But just the fact that a celebrity has gone out to dinner isn't very interesting.

Some press agents try to get around the fact that nothing has happened while celebrities are eating at their restaurants by linking unrelated newsworthy information to the celebrity, and the restaurant, which leads to items like: "Milton Berle reveals to Anthony Quinn over pasta at Il Bozo that Prince will star in a revival of *The Music Man.*"

Milton Berle and Anthony Quinn may have eaten dinner at Il Bozo, but it probably wasn't to discuss Prince or *The Music Man.* These sorts of items are very popular with old-time press agents. It's a way of simultaneously getting in a restaurant plug while imparting what actually may be newsworthy information. I shy away from them, however, knowing that many of them are partial, if not total, fiction.

There is a restaurant in New York called Nirvana, which employs a press agent of the old school, Sy Presten. If you believe Presten, you'd have to believe Nirvana doesn't need a press agent because every other day he calls to inform you that yet another couple of celebrities have stopped by to sample the exotic cuisine. They usually say something newsworthy during dinner as well. If there are that many celebrities jamming the place, then why is the restaurant looking for press? Often the celebrities dining at Nirvana, like Penthouse publisher Bob Guccione or divorce attorney Marvin Mitchelson, are also clients of Presten's. He is not above going for the gusto, trying to promote two or three clients in one fell swoop of a column item.

One night at a dinner party at the disco Area, I was seated next to actor Christopher Reeve. "You work at the *Post,*" he said. "Maybe you can explain something." Reeve said his name had appeared in a gossip column in the *Post* (thank God, it hadn't been Page Six) as having lunched with Calvin Klein, and that, according to the gossip column, they had discussed his next movie. "I've been in that restaurant," said Reeve. "But not to have lunch with Calvin Klein, and not to talk about a movie. Where do they get that stuff?"

I tried to explain to him the science of restaurant press agentry, but I don't think he grasped the concept.

The presence of certain celebrities at restaurants or nightclubs is news, but a gossip columnist has to be careful not to fall for phony lists of names. They key phrase is "expected to attend." If a press agent looking to promote an event calls to say "The Pope, Frank Sinatra and Jackie Onassis are expected to attend," the press agent isn't really lying. Maybe invitations have been sent, and it is hoped Frank, Jackie and the Pope will show up. If they don't, it's not the press agent's fault, right?

I run occasional spot checks on these press agents, by showing up at the party, or sending someone from the staff. If the "expected" guest list is unusually stellar, and the only celebrity to show is Sylvia Miles, who isn't even on the list, we temporarily blacklist the press agent from the column until the press agent has been properly chastened.

Sometimes, the press agent isn't to blame. If a gossip column runs an item saying Mick Jagger and Robert De Niro are expected at a party, the two stars may have intended to go, but will cancel after the story appears, fearing too much media attention.

Lists of celebrities at parties make for fairly boring reading, but are necessary once in a while to pay back press agents who've been helpful with "non-client" information. These are the intelligent press agents. If a press agent gives me two or three good items completely unrelated to clients, I'm willing to help out with a client plug. Certain press agents go overboard in this department, like the one who, soon after I started at Page Six, said to me, "Sweetie, let me teach you about press agent quid pro quo. I give you an item, you plug my client. Got it?"

Even if I owe a press agent a favor, I demand an angle—and a truthful one—to go with the client plug. If it involves a restaurant, some sort of an event has to have taken place there, anything other than a dull list of names.

If asked, I certainly wouldn't need my toes, and probably not even all ten fingers, to count off the press agents I trust and get along with. The ones I do consider professional are enormously helpful; the rest do nothing but contribute to the "flack attack."

When all the phone lines on Page Six were jammed with press agents pushing items, I would put the lines on hold, slap my hands over my ears and yell, "Flack attack!" Then I'd go to the cafeteria or ladies' room and let someone else deal with it.

The press agents' opening pitches are crucial in determining whether or not they will be taken seriously. At the *Post,* the ones who opened with, "Excuse me, can you tell me who writes Page Six?" or "What kind of column is Page Six?" were automatically disqualified. If they didn't even read the column, I didn't have time for them.

Also not to be taken seriously are those who ask, "What kind of an angle do I need to get in the column? Can you think of one?" I'm not getting paid to sit around concocting angles for public relations people.

Then there are the true bullshit artists: "Baby, have I got an exclusive for you! A world exclusive! And if you're not going to run it, you've got to let me know—right now! The other columns are clamoring for it!" In that case, I tell the press agent, I feel awful about depriving the other columnists and perhaps he should call them instead.

I am decidedly wary as well of press agents who open

their pitch with, "I have got the cutest item for you. It is so adorable you're not going to believe it!" These items invariably involve somebody doing something nice, fun and/or darling with little kiddies, senior citizens and/or furry pets. They are so sweet, I slip into sugar shock and find myself unable to cope with the story or the press agent.

Honesty is always appreciated. If a flack for a movie studio calls and admits, "This one's a total dog, but I could really use a little press on it," I'm more apt to consider a story about the dreadful film, particularly if the press agent is a cooperative one, than if the flack calls and says, of the same canine cinematic effort, "It's the finest film I've ever seen in my life and you'd be a fool not to write about it."

Once I received a note from a public relations executive who knew most of the Page Six staff. He was suggesting an item about a political fund raiser:

"All right, I know it's nothing but a bunch of neo-fascists down there, but I've got a deal for you. I'll subtract two Hampton weekends, add three saki and beer tastings, and throw in a tennis lesson if you can figure out a way to write this thing up. I will also pull the plug on my nearly total self-imposed silence and come up with some real items. Who wants to go to an unbelievable party tomorrow night?"

I liked this guy's approach. We ran the item.

Certain individual press agents stand out as singularly entertaining characters.

Harvey Mann, a former actor and later head of casting for 20th Century-Fox, now runs his own public relations operation, and over the years has represented a mixed bag of clients, including such individuals as Joe Namath and

Mariel Hemingway, discos like Studio 54, and later the Palladium, and restaurants, including Hisae's, the River Café and Sam's. On dark days, a call to Mann sheds ridiculous light on the whole business. Though serious about promoting his clients, Mann turns everything else into a delightfully absurd process.

Mann is fond of the flamboyant gesture and the sweeping statement. "There's no queen like an old queen," he regularly declares, or "She's so tacky she makes me look like Grace Kelly." Working out of his apartment on the Upper East Side ("I haven't left the house since Judy died"), Mann cooks while he works, his work consisting primarily of calls to clients or to columnists and other journalists. Often when I call, he is preparing something— macaroni and cheese, brisket of beef, chicken soup. When visiting friends in the country, says Mann, "You'll find me in the kitchen in my dimity apron putting up the preserves."

He does leave his apartment occasionally, once for a trip to California, where he met Lana Turner, attired in a bold caftan, at a party. What did they talk about, I asked? Mann reported that he'd said to her "Lana, my sex life should be as busy as your dress . . . and yours has been."

At the same party, Mann said, he chatted with an older man who years earlier had been a leading hairdresser in Hollywood. Once, a young actress whose mane the hairdresser was in the process of taming, died while under the drier. It's considered very bad form to bring up the tragic accident, but Mann didn't know this. He suggested the hairdresser, who undoubtedly had dozens of star stories to tell, write a book. Mann said he could call the chapter

about the death of the young actress "The Last Wave."
Shortly after this, the hairdresser exited the party.

The day after John Lennon was killed, Mann went totally out of control. Jim Brady, who was editing the column then, got a call from Mann insisting that Lennon,
before he died, had made frequent trips to Hisae's restaurant, across the street from his apartment building. "He
loved the chocolate cake," said Mann, weeping into the
receiver. "It was his favorite dessert." Then he added: "If
you run the item, don't forget to mention Hisae's, on West
Seventy-second."

An even more outrageous character is Bobby Zarem, a
frenzied press agent with mostly show business clients.
He handles a number of individuals, including Michael
Caine, Jackie Collins and Alan Alda, and frequently works
on movie campaigns.

Looking alarmingly like Larry of the Three Stooges with
his fringe of curly hair, disheveled attire and portly figure,
Zarem makes frequent phone calls to columnists, but is
better known for his letters, which can run up to twelve
typed pages, always extolling the unheard of peaks
reached by his clients. When he was working on Brian de
Palma's film *Scarface,* Zarem's letter predicted the movie,
which thrilled neither audiences nor critics, "without a
doubt" would be "the biggest box office hit of the year"
and would "sweep the Oscars . . . I predict with at least
eleven nominations."

Zarem is quite direct in describing what he feels is his
considerable weight. In one letter, he wrote, "I am the top
public relations company in this country having, among
other things, spent three and a half years of my life creating and then executing what became the 'I LOVE NEW YORK'

campaign which literally saved New York and a great deal of the people, institutions and businesses in it."

Zarem is big on creating publicity events. When the Three Mile Island disaster occurred, Zarem was coordinating publicity for *The China Syndrome,* a film focusing on a similar mishap at a nuclear plant. Every entertainment writer in New York was convinced that Zarem had engineered Three Mile Island to coincide with the movie's opening. It was supposed to be a joke, but with Zarem, who knew?

When promoting the film version of the Broadway thriller *Deathtrap,* Zarem, in the tones of his native Savannah, called to say the film "reeked of Oscar" and contained performances that were "lahk shooting bullets at ya. They ah among the fahnest Ah have ever seen in mah entah-er career."

Zarem, who operates in an extremely frazzled state, occasionally gets on my nerves and causes me to lose all patience with him. The first time this happened, he threatened to jump off the Brooklyn Bridge if I didn't write something about a client he was plugging: "It could mean mah career! Mah lahf!" Tired of his hysteria, I didn't speak to him for several months, but eventually forgot about our fight. There is no point in staying peeved at Zarem for a prolonged period of time. He's too amusing, and besides, he's got a lot of good clients.

There are press agents who specialize in rock stars, others in society figures. Politicians all have press agents, referred to as press secretaries. The presence of press agents is so pervasive that direct calls to newsworthy figures often are automatically referred to a press agent. There are may ways to find out who represents whom, but when seeking the notable or notorious, Celebrity Service is the most efficient.

A research and contact service headquartered in New York, Celebrity Service employs a staff trained to field calls from news organizations and others who regularly contact celebrities. If I have to get in touch with a writer, an actor or even a deposed dictator, I call Celebrity Service for the phone numbers they have on file, usually a press agent, an agent, a lawyer or a manager. I think of it as a huge up-to-date Rolodex.

Press agents are certainly not a new breed. At the heyday of the Hollywood studio system, there were plenty of press agents toiling in studio publicity departments, assigned to constructing images for stars—often diametrically opposed to the stars' true personas. The image-making continues, and has spread into the new fields of celebrity.

Today, the political image makers are the most powerful. Though most political media consultants would bristle at comparison with press agents, the roles are similar—presenting an image to the press, and the public.

Actually, political media consultants are a combination of press agent, advertising executive and producer. They not only present the image, but literally construct it as well through the television commercials that may make or break a candidate.

Integral in the political process, media consultants are used by the press as experts in political analysis, and often are quoted in newspapers or interviewed on television. With ever-growing public profiles, they've become celebrities themselves. Gossip columns like Page Six and "Inside New York" frequently write about the consultants as well as the candidates.

In the office of one prominent Washington consultant, Robert Squier, whose candidates run the gamut from would-be congressmen to would-be presidents, a notice once was posted regarding interoffice memos: "Put nothing on paper you would not be comfortable seeing on the front page of the New York Times or (more likely) Page Six of the New York Post . . . If it is on paper, it will find its way into the paper."

Often, I've wondered what my job—or any media job for that matter—would be like without image makers of any kind. What if there were no flacks or press agents or consultants, and all celebrities and personalities were exposed in their raw forms to media scrutiny? What if they all went to interviews alone, without a press adviser by their sides to kick them under the table whenever something inappropriate to their assigned images was said?

Given the number of journalists seeking access to certain public figures, there is an impractical side to eliminating the middle man, and yet there is also the intriguing prospect that such unencumbered encounters would be more informative, and entertaining, for the press, for the public and for the personalities themselves.

Press agents also function as refining agents, and what they place on a platter for media observation and analysis is a well-polished piece of a celebrity. The piece is frequently quite small, and not representative of the whole, with the quirky, and more interesting, bumps lopped off in the process. In the course of writing about celebrities, it's impossible to avoid the influence of refining press agents, but there's ample opportunity to glimpse certain celebrities without their shields. Some are confident enough to say what they feel without prior consultation, and even the most image conscious can inadvertently expose their true selves. Some celebrities even fit their images.

One of the perks that comes with the job of gossip columnist is a good table at Elaine's. It shouldn't matter where you are seated in a restaurant, I tell myself, and Elaine's is no different from any other restaurant. Yeah, right. Despite my lofty resolves to avoid falling into such traps, I get a major charge out of Elaine's, which is usually packed with writers, directors, actors, producers and Woody Allen.

One night I went to the restaurant with a group of five or six people. We were placed at a large table near the back of the front room, right opposite a table for two, at which Shirley MacLaine was seated with another woman. Their heads together as we walked by, MacLaine and her companion obviously were engaged in a serious conversation of some sort.

Consistently amazed at MacLaine's outrageous pronouncements on reincarnation and communication with spirits, I considered her the ultimate space cadet.

Never having interviewed her myself, I had wondered then if the whole cosmic tourist image wasn't a scam, something she, or an astute press agent, had constructed to cast her in an out-of-this-world light.

We ordered drinks, then dinner and were having a fine time, when MacLaine's companion got up and passed by our table en route to the ladies room. I suppose she was gone for several minutes, but I wasn't really paying that much attention.

I did notice, however, since my seat was up against the wall and faced MacLaine's table, that she was staring intently at our group. Again, I didn't pay it much mind, chalking up my observation to paranoia.

After MacLaine's friend had returned to their table, I directed a comment to the person sitting opposite me. He held out his hand to interrupt. "Give me a minute," he said. "I'm doing some very interesting eavesdropping."

This sounded good. As the rest of us finished our meal, we speculated upon what he was overhearing.

A few minutes later, his listening finished, he drew in his chair.

"Well, well," he said. "Miss MacLaine has just analyzed our table."

Moments before her friend returned to MacLaine's table, a waiter had arrived at ours with one dessert. I hadn't ordered dessert, and neither had the other woman seated at our table. Her boyfriend had, so we took our spoons and dove into his.

According to MacLaine, said our eavesdropper, the two women at our table were extremely undignifed, as was illustrated by the manner in which we made a pass at someone else's dessert. And, he added, MacLaine had observed an air of lasciviousness pervading the entire table. We looked around at one other for previously undetected signs of lewdness.

Finally, he reported, MacLaine said she had somehow detected that someone at our table was brain-damaged. We pressed for further details: Who was the brain-damaged one? He claimed she hadn't specifically pointed out the mentally deficient member of our party, but we argued that she probably had and he was being polite, not wanting to embarrass the retard.

We had a long discussion about how she had reached these conclusions. Had she known some of us in previous lives? When she was Cleopatra, maybe one of us had been Antony? Had she perhaps worked in a mental institution in the nineteenth-century, when one, or maybe more that one of us, had been admitted with Civil War wounds so extensive that brain surgery was required? Or had she based her conclusions solely on twentieth-century dessert-eating observations?

There were many options to consider, but one conclusion I'd already reached was that MacLaine did not need a press agent to construct an image for her. Her self-motivated weirdness was certainly sufficient.

Chapter 7

SOCIALITES LEAP FROM POSH PADS

Arianna Stassinopoulos is an expert climber of social mountains. She stands before them undaunted, straps on her gear and begins scaling the often formidable promontories. It is an awesome spectacle.

While a student at Cambridge University, Stassinopoulos, also a writer, formed alliances with men who were long on influence, including *Times* of London columnist Bernard Levin and, later, publisher George Weidenfeld. Armed with introductions from the contacts she'd made in Britain, Stassinopoulos moved to New York. In virtually no time at all, she had made a mark on the higher echelons of New York society, primarily through her lavish dinner parties, which were attended by the likes of Placido Domingo and Françoise de la Renta. Suddenly, Stassinopoulos was sharing private fitness sessions with Barbara Walters, and Ann Getty was her best friend.

Undoubtedly, there are dozens of instances of young men or women arriving in New York laden with introductions from abroad, but few can lay claim to the swift social success achieved by Stassinopoulos. What caused her to stand apart? Technique may have had something to do with it.

At a cocktail party, while talking to someone she has concluded will be of minimal use to her, Stassinopoulos focuses not on that feckless individual, but on the rest of the room, which she works with her eyes, darting away swiftly upon noticing someone else in the crowd of more importance or influence.

Stassinopoulos is tall—close to six feet—so she can scan a room quickly, with only a few perceptible jerks of the head and neck. The jerks stop suddenly when she lights upon her prey, and for just a moment she stands up straight and rigid, then strides forward to meet them. Her movements are ostrich-like, only instead of sticking her head in the sand, she sticks it, face first, in front of the hopefully influential and powerful person she has chosen to chat up. And, once she's made a hit, Stassinopoulos doesn't let go. She keeps in touch with her conquests, placing regular phone calls and sending gifts on special occasions.

Working the after-hours beat in New York, I've become familiar with numerous, disparate social playing fields, from the glaring sights and sounds of a new wave club on Avenue A to the less frenzied, but often just as glaring, maneuverings, at a cocktail party on Manhattan's Upper East Side. The latter was Stassinopoulos's turf, until she reached a personal peak—her very own Mount Everest— by marrying a Texas millionaire introduced by climbing connections.

I've come to be familiar with other players on the social fields as well, many of whom create themselves in the middle of sporting events. Manhattan is a setting in which it's easy to eliminate the restraining ties of background and birth. Those eager to join most of the social athletic teams are not loaded down with historical equipment. The one exception is the team known as Old Money. For that, background and birth are all that matter.

One such self-created figure is Patricia Kluge. Wed to John Kluge, who sold his Metromedia broadcast empire to Rupert Murdoch for close to $2 billion, Patricia Kluge certainly didn't take to announcing at cocktail parties that she'd once posed in compromising positions for a skin magazine in England. The information was irrelevant to her American goals, and didn't emerge until several years after she'd already soared to impressive heights here. And, at that point, her trophies were bolted down and irretrievable.

Nigel Dempster, England's most well-known gossip columnist, was the one who originally exposed Patricia Kluge's background in his column in London's *Daily Mail.* Eventually, the information that Kluge was, as Dempster put it, "a former Baghdad-born, of British origin, belly dancer, who dispensed sex under her name in a raunchy, men-only magazine" made it over to New York.

During an interview I did with Dempster, the topic of Kluge came up. He said someone like her "who now represents herself as something else, should be exposed. As I would expect to be exposed if I was once a closet queen who suborned young boys in Picadilly. The British have got an age-old knowledge that if you do something wrong, it'll be exposed. It may not, but it can be. . . .You can't be Jay Gatsby. It would last about two and a half seconds."

Not so in New York, where a would-be socialite who mentally forms a self-image can quickly construct a being to match. There are dozens of Jay Gatsbys. There are just as many Athenas floating around town, all sprung from the foreheads of unknown Zeuses.

The socialites are from everywhere, and from nowhere at the same time. The fact that they are in Manhattan, displaying their social skills, is all that figures in the final tally. Some have parents and other relatives, but these relatives are produced only if they've proven suitably dexterous.

It's difficult to fix an image through surroundings. Most parties and events are held in impersonal venues—clubs, hotels, restaurants. It's not unheard of for Manhattan's terribly social to entertain at home, but it's certainly not the norm.

When covering parties, I am transformed myself—from a gossip columnist into a sports writer, dutifully recording the play-by-play. When it turns to blood sports, it can be gut-wrenching, but I grit my teeth and forge on.

Never overly competent at party reporting, but resigned to it, I've attempted to form a working strategy.

In my early years at Page Six, before I was named editor, I didn't worry all that much about my party demeanor. If I attended a function and got a story out of it, fine. If I was too nervous to talk to anybody, well, the events would continue, the column would survive and so would I. Basically, nobody would notice.

My pattern at that point was to walk into a room and immediately case it for familiar faces. If I spotted one, I would latch onto it, and hang on tenaciously. Sometimes the familiar face would try to ditch me with subtle footwork: "Excuse me just a minute. I'm going to run over to the bar." Did I fall for that? Heck no. I'd say: "I'd like another drink myself. I'll go with you."

If a familiar face failed to present itself, I would stand in a corner talking to the ice cubes in my drink.

Sometimes I would bring a friend along as a safety measure, but that never worked out very well. If the friend knew no one either, then the two of us would stand there talking to each other. It would suddenly occur to us that we could be anywhere—perhaps in some nice familiar restaurant, having dinner—and so we'd leave, wondering why we'd bothered to come in the first place.

Once I became the editor, I figured it might be wise to formulate a different strategy. Nipping at the heels of familiar faces and chatting with ice cubes were behavior patterns unlikely to enhance the content, or the reputation, of the column.

My revitalized game plan was two-pronged. Section A: walk into a room and look for familiar faces. Okay, that part of it wasn't much different from the old strategy, but, according to the new rules, if I found a familiar face, I was only allowed to talk to it for a few minutes, just until I was able to get over those first few minutes of party panic. Then, Section B would go into effect: find two celebrities and talk to them. I didn't have to talk to them for long— just introduce myself and say something insightful like: "Some party, huh?" or "What are you doing here?" Occasionally a mini-conversation would follow, perhaps containing a quotable comment. If not, I'd just say "Nice to meet you" and rush back to the familiar face until I was ready to approach the second celebrity and repeat Section B.

Fouls were frequent, like the time I approached Paul Newman at a press party, momentarily forgetting his disdain for the *Post*. He glared at me and said, "I don't like your newspaper or your newspaper's owner and I don't have to talk to you." The ice cubes had been friendlier, if not more forthcoming.

At other times, an informative discussion would emerge. At a party following a benefit dance performance, I went up to Paul Simon. He said he'd read and liked a story I'd written about a radio station owned by him and his brother. I asked what he was up to, and his response resulted in an item for the column.

Approaching celebrities and talking to them did not qualify them for the familar faces category. Most failed to remember me if I ran into them a second or third time, not surprising given the number of journalists floating around parties in New York. And there were many like Arianna Stassinopoulos, who might have met a person three dozen times, but would only recall potentially useful faces, which is why Stassinopoulos's techniques were so fascinating to observe.

On the downtown end of the social scale, Diane Brill is Stassinopoulos's equivalent. Brill, a fashion designer whose true calling is socializing, is also tall, and large. Blond and buxom is a description that doesn't do her justice. In Brill's arena, whatever clubs are momentarily hot, it's too dark to visually work a room effectively, and too loud to hear anything. Conversations in clubs rarely yield material for the column, but all the smiling—the only way to react when you have no idea what's just been said— makes the atmosphere seem much more civilized.

Uptown, downtown, midtown—no field ever has become what I'd call comfortable, but I hang in there, presuming that, eventually, a number of the athletes will become familiar faces, and it will all be much easier. Also, after doing this for a while, I've become a sort of sports fan, with favorites for whom I root.

Brill is one of my favorites. You have to give credit to a person who will go into the game with that outrageous a uniform—hair teased to the sky, and rubber dresses into which someone in the locker room obviously has poured her. And she has a sense of irony about the sports—rare in social athletes, most of whom are as deadly serious as Vince Lombardi when it comes to winning. Stassinopoulos was one of the serious ones, but I cheered her on nonetheless, if only because I admired her sheer bravado. She orchestrated her own wedding as a sort of social Super Bowl. As the fashion newspaper *Women's Wear Daily* noted, "Almost every pew had its very own syndicated gossip columnist."

There was one face not confined to a specific geographical area of New York's social fields who played as expertly at a cocktail party at Mortimer's as at an East Village art opening: Andy Warhol. Actually, the reason Warhol fit in everywhere was that he was more of an observer than a player. He was the ultimate sports fan. He even wore a uniform that suited all occasions and events: black. Once Warhol became a familiar face, things became much easier.

You couldn't miss him. With his shock of platinum hair and his pale, seemingly lifeless countenance, he resembled a human Etch-A-Sketch, a silvery TV-like screen, which, with a twist or two of its controlling knobs, suddenly is covered with a self-propelled design. A smart shake erases the design, returning it to its blank state.

He seemed to absorb everything around him, and incorporate it into his art. His greatest artistic creation was probably himself—and a protean piece of work at that. Warhol helped change the times, and changed with them, all the while remaining what he had created, which, was, simply, Warhol.

Warhol was born the son of a coal mine worker in Pittsburgh, but he never talked much about the old days, at least not to me. I knew of his mother, because he once had lived with her, but I wasn't aware he had two brothers until after his death.

Warhol didn't seem to mind being latched onto, and I took advantage of this fact, hanging on with a vulcan death grip if a social situation was particularly intimidating.

My dread of attending celebrity functions dissipated if Warhol happened to be there. He often happened to be there. He seemed to go out more than anyone in New York, fulfilling a need he once described as a "social disease." A party didn't seem to be a party until he'd arrived. Warhol was a referee as well as a fan. When he walked into a party, his presence seemed to proclaim: "Play ball!" Since his death in February 1987, party-hopping in New York has lost some of its energy. So has gossip. Socializing and gossiping were two of his passions.

It could even be said that he'd had a formative influence on the current state of the gossip column. As the godfather of pop art, Warhol was instrumental not only in contributing to art forms in the traditional sense, but in fashioning a lifestyle as art, the celebrity lifestyle. I'm not sure how well regarded this art form will be in the twenty-third, twenty-second or even the twenty-first century, but in the here and now it contributes to the definition of what is hot and what is not, and which players make features in *People* magazine or in Warhol's *Interview,* and which languish in anonymity. The games, after all, are played primarily with one goal in mind: attention. The media hand out most of the medals.

Many of the celebrities whose activities are chronicled in gossip columns are products of the type of celebrity assembly line Warhol originated at the Factory in the 1960s. The Superstars of that era were the original celebrities for celebrity's sake: Edie Sedgwick, Ultra Violet, Baby Jane Holzer, Viva. They didn't labor at learning a skill, earning recognition when their talents reached a peak. They were instant, overnight, disposable celebrities. Few remember their specific achievements, when there were any. The fact that they were Superstars is the accomplishment on record.

My first real introduction to Warhol was through Maura Moynihan, one of the last of his Superstar-like discoveries, the novas who burst out of nowhere to recognition through the Warhol connection. Other than the family name—her father is the senator from New York—there wasn't much known about Moynihan when Warhol decided to put her on the cover of his *Interview* magazine in the summer of 1981. But Moynihan rated a cover, for the simple reason that Warhol thought she was hot. "I was a little nobody," Moynihan recalls. "Andy believed in me when nobody else did."

Warhol was delighted when Moynihan, who was also pursuing careers as an actress and singer, took a job working two days a week on Page Six. He enjoyed gossip, and was particularly partial to the camp sensibilities of the New York *Post.* He saw the *Post,* as did many of the "downtown" artists, as its own peculiar art form. The mix of screaming headlines, rabidly right-wing editorials and gossip—lots of gossip—made it must reading.

And so Warhol and I became friends, and occasional

party partners. My friendship with Warhol was a working relationship. When we'd go out, it would be to have a good time, but also to gather material—I for the column, he for his art work, or his magazine. He was also on the lookout for photo opportunities and never went anywhere without a camera. The evenings I spent out on the town with him in New York were always memorable.

The fact that Warhol was a celebrity himself had a lot to do with it. If I was working the social circuit with him, there was little chance that my being a columnist would make some other notable nervous. I was just another member of Warhol's entourage: "If she's with Andy, she must be okay."

Playing the social field—hitting the events, openings and other extravaganzas that clutter the calendars of media-wise New Yorkers—was a lot more enjoyable with Warhol around, if only because he actually thought it was fun. Not very many of the players ever see the games for what they're really worth, a few laughs. But Warhol retained a wide-eyed incredulity at the circles in which he'd spun for years. His observations often were punctuated with comments like: "Oh, god, this is so greeaaaaat. Can you believe how many stars are here?"

Warhol was aware that his urge to socialize had become a joke to some. I ran into him the night after he'd attended a party celebrating the unveiling of a renovated section of a department store. "Everybody says I'd go to the opening of an envelope," he commented. "Well, last night I went to the opening of an escalator at Bergdorf's. That's almost as good as an envelope."

There was a deadly serious side to his socializing as well. Though he was invited to just about every major event held in New York, he worried when he felt he'd been left out of something.

Malcolm Forbes and his family are renowned for their lavish parties. For a time, the Forbes's guest lists regularly featured Warhol's name. Then, suddenly, they didn't. Warhol was mystified as to why he'd been dropped from the Forbes's social register.

"They used to invite me all the time," he said. "But the last couple of parties, no invitation."

With the amount of socializing he did, I couldn't believe Warhol was bothered by missing a party here or there. But the Forbes's parties are not run-of-the-mill events, and always draw a mix of celebrities from a variety of fields— media, business, the arts, society and so on.

Warhol surmised that he'd been dropped because a crasher used his name to get into a party on the Forbes yacht.

"He said he was with me, and they let him in," Andy explained. "But he wasn't with me."

If he was really bothered by it, I suggested, why didn't he call one of Malcolm Forbes's sons and ask what was wrong.

"Oh no," he said. "I could never do that."

He couldn't be that upset by it, I told myself, but he must have been because he mentioned it to me three or four times.

Several months later, I ran into him at a party on the Forbes's floating pleasure palace.

"I guess I'm finally out of Siberia," he said, adding that he'd never figured out, definitively, what he'd done to be dropped, or brought back on board.

It was impossible to make fun of Warhol, because he always made fun of himself. Every place he traveled, every event he attended, every person he met was "greeaaaaat." I asked Warhol once about a ballet he'd been to, a matinee of *The Nutcracker.* He pronounced it "greaaaat. All those little rich kids!" Some time before that, at the opening of the abysmal John Travolta-Sylvester Stallone collaboration, *Stayin' Alive,* I emerged from the theater with a splitting headache from the *dreck* I'd just seen on the screen. "Oh, God," said Warhol. "I loved it. All those gorgeous kids. They were so greeeaaaat." To Warhol, what was good was good, but what was bad was even better— particularly if it contained one or all of the three elements that seemed to intrigue him the most: youth, wealth and beauty.

In 1985, right around the time professional wrestling was being transformed from a hugely popular entertainment, but one largely ignored by the mainstream media, to a chic sort of happening involving other sorts of celebrities, a friend of mine who was a longtime devotee said he'd seen Warhol in the front row at Madison Square Garden for a Monday-night wrestling card. I called Warhol for his impressions, intending to write a story declaring wrestling officially "in" now that he'd discovered it. "It's hip, it's exciting, it's America," he said, describing the mat men as "real big beauties." Warhol suggested we get tickets for the next event, which MTV planned to broadcast live. "Everyone will be there," he said. "Cyndi Lauper, Mr. T."

It was the most theatrically satisfying event I'd attended in some time. The frenzy of the crowd reached a level I'd seen only once before, at a Bruce Springsteen concert. At one point, all the wrestlers and all the special celebrity guests jumped into the ring for a free-for-all.

When the match ended—and Hulk Hogan had assumed

the heavyweight title—we went backstage. There were many ominous-looking men with thick necks hanging around. Warhol was supposed to go on camera for MTV, but things seemed to be slightly disorganized so we stood waiting near the entrance to the dressing rooms. One of the WWF staff came over and said he had someone who wanted to meet Warhol. It was Mrs. Hulk Hogan.

Mrs. Hulk was quite the hot number, with bleached blond hair, a mini-skirt and a fake fur coat. "I can't believe it's you," she said to Warhol. "I can't believe it either," he responded.

I asked Mrs. Hulk how she'd met her husband. She revealed that she'd first made his acquaintance at a bar in California. "Don't let anyone ever tell you you can't meet guys in bars," she advised. "Because I did."

"She is so greeaaaaat," said Warhol, who suggested we all have lunch at a later date. Mrs. Hulk was also very taken with Warhol and asked to have her photo snapped standing next to him, even though, she hastened to assure us, this wasn't her first brush with fame. "I know all about celebrities," she said. "My sister is an actress and she was on 'T. J. Hooker.' "

Warhol often traveled with a group of people, sometimes members of his staff or friends, or *Interview*'s Paige Powell, who fit both descriptions and who was his most constant nightlife companion during the last years of his life. If I'd made plans to go out with him, I never knew who else might be joining us—or what sort of activity we'd be covering. It could be wrestling, but then again, we might end up sipping cocktails on Park Avenue.

I hadn't seen Warhol for a while when I ran into him at a party at the Palladium. We made plans to get together for dinner later that week.

He called the next morning with a change in plans. He'd forgotten about the Bob Dylan and Tom Petty concert. He was supposed to take photographs. Did I want to accompany him to that, rather than go out to dinner? Sure, I said, why not? Warhol told me I should meet him at his office. "The car will be here at seven-fifteen," he said.

I liked the sound of that. Nothing like running around town in a limo.

Detained by a last-minute emergency at the office, I was ten or fifteen minutes late. When I arrived at Warhol's studio, one of his assistants said Warhol would be down momentarily. He and Vincent Fremont, who helped run the Warhol businesses, were taking Paulina and Rick on a tour.

"Who are Paulina and Rick?" I asked.

You know, said the assistant, the model Paulina, and "Rick" was really Ric, Ric Ocasek, of the rock group The Cars.

Because Ocasek had arrived in a limo at the appointed hour, I'm still not certain if Warhol meant The Car, or the car, when he said the vehicle would be at his office at seven-fifteen.

The nice thing about being part of a group that includes Paulina Porizkova is not having to worry about what to wear. It doesn't really make much difference. She is not one of those fashion models who, off the job, resembles any old female. At all times, Paulina turns heads.

So does Ocasek, who is pale, thin and tall. Real tall, like about a foot taller than anyone else. Paulina's mother, who looked about five years older than Paulina, was also along for the show. She was in from Sweden for a visit and didn't speak much English.

Presumably because Ocasek had played the Garden,

and knew the ropes, the limo didn't leave us outside the arena, but drove right into the bowels of the place, depositing us at the entrance to the backstage area. We walked around for a while, observing the various roadies, then went in and took our seats.

When the concert was over, we all trooped backstage, I guess to talk to Dylan, but he didn't seem to be emerging. In the hall outside the dressing rooms, there was a manager here, a tour manager there, Dylan's mother here and lots of roadies everywhere. There was no air-conditioning anywhere. I couldn't figure out what anyone was doing, except sweating. It was a typical summer night in New York—ninety-nine degrees, humid, no ventilation. Only Paulina, who was wearing full makeup, remained dry. Vincent Fremont finally asked her what her secret was.

"When you are a model, and are standing under hot lights all the time, you learn how not to sweat," she said. "I never sweat."

Warhol thought she was "greeaaat." Ditto Ocasek, the concert, the backstage area and the limo ride uptown to a restaurant where a post-concert dinner was to be held.

Soon after we arrived at the restaurant, I told Warhol I'd have to get going. It was already after midnight and I had to be at work early the next day.

"Don't you want to talk to Bob?" asked Warhol.

Well, that would be kind of nice, I said, but judging by the time it has taken Dylan to make a brief appearance outside his dressing room, it would probably be 2 A.M. before he arrived at the restaurant.

"But how can you leave now?" asked Warhol, with a distinct note of disbelief. "He's sooooo famous."

Though no slouch himself in the fame department, Warhol sounded genuinely awed when he made comments like this. Despite his own notoriety, he couldn't believe he was hanging out with whom he was hanging out.

Warhol was so fond of social games, he even turned the midday meal into a party, hosting regular luncheons at his headquarters.

By the time I met him, Warhol had moved the Factory, his studio and other offices, to its third site, in a building on Union Square. The lunches were often business-oriented, with *Interview* advertisers among the guests, and an artsy downtown personality or two thrown in for spice. Salads and other healthy sorts of foods would be served. Warhol, who'd come close to death when Valerie Solanas shot him in 1968, was concerned with physical fitness. He worked out regularly with a personal trainer, popped vitamins religiously and adhered to a mostly health food-type diet, though he did have a sweet tooth and would succumb to "just one bite" of certain irresistible desserts.

For one lunch at the Factory, I arrived early. Wandering around the rooms, which were packed to the rafters with paintings, furniture and all manner of artistic bric-a-brac, I came across Jean-Michel Basquiat, one of the young artists for whom Warhol served as mentor, on his hands and knees working on a rough canvas material covered with primitive sketches of what appeared to be dogs, or dog-like animals. Basquiat was drawing small shapeless things near the animals. Actually, it looked like he was drawing dog droppings, but I didn't want to say so, just in case they weren't. "Aren't those nice!" I commented.

Basquiat looked up at me and said, with no little disdain: "Andy did dogs. I did piss and shit."

"Oh well, they're awfully nice," I said.

Wherever he went, Warhol carried a stack of copies of

Interview, the magazine he started in 1969. In its early years, *Interview* was remarkable for the length of its features, which appeared to go to press without the touch of an editing hand. Transcripts of tapes were published complete with all extraneous matter, which would lead to long passages about things like spinach salad: Had it been ordered and who wanted it?

Warhol asked the questions for some of the stories himself, usually at one of his lunches with the aid of a co-interviewer. Sometimes, a celebrity would turn the tables on him. In 1980, he and Tatum O'Neal had a chat about love.

O'NEAL: You can't help it when it happens. You're not in control.

WARHOL: Really?

O'NEAL: True. You don't think so?

WARHOL: Kids are the ones who fall in love.

O'NEAL: Are you kidding? That's not true. You'll meet somebody. You just have to get out of the crowd you hang around with. You'll meet her, I promise.

WARHOL: Where? In the subway?

O'NEAL: Don't you want to have a little Andy Warhol?

WARHOL: No.

In late '83, he asked me if I was interested in participating in an interview for a Goldie Hawn cover story.

Hawn and her p.r. man, Alan Eichorn, came down to the Factory for the lunch. It wasn't just the four of us. Warhol's dermatologist was there, and also his personal trainer. At one point, the interview lapsed into a long discussion about fitness, skin and makeup, which didn't have anything to do with the interesting stuff we should have been trying to get Hawn to talk about—like her boyfriend Kurt Russell.

Bringing up movie stars' personal lives often leads to defensive reactions, so I tried to think of some subtle way to broach the topic. It wasn't necessary. Warhol did it in a distinctly unsubtle fashion by noting that he'd just seen Russell in a movie, and, boy, was he ever cute.

Despite the occasional off-the-wall question or comment, Warhol was an effective interviewer. Perhaps because he was a celebrity himself, he could get people to talk about things they might have avoided if Seymour Hersh had been asking the questions, and the fact that the interviews took place as part of a casual luncheon made it all the easier.

We used Warhol's tape recorder for the interview. When the end of the first half of the tape was reached, the recorder was supposed to switch automatically to the second. After Hawn had left, Warhol looked at the recorder.

"Oh no," he said. "It never switched to the second side."

I'd made some notes during the lunch, but not many. I quickly attempted to reconstruct quotes from them, and to recall what else Hawn had said of importance the last hour of the interview. I couldn't remember all that much.

I suggested one of us call her and explain what had happened, then ask a few questions over the phone. Warhol was horrified at the suggestion.

"We can't do that," he said. "She's such a big star."

I turned in a transcript of what we had—not the most scintillating stuff ever to see print, although I like one comment from Warhol: "I think land is the best art, if you don't put anything on it."

Most of my socializing with Warhol involved events of some sort, but occasionally we would skip the extravaganzas and just go to a screening or a restaurant. Whenever someone asked me "But isn't he incredibly boring?" I would say: no, though he did have his dull moments.

One night, he and I met at a Broadway screening room for a preview of *True Stories,* the directorial debut of David Byrne of the Talking Heads. Both fans of Byrne's flat, deadpan style—a style Warhol pioneered—we'd heard positive advance word on the movie and were eager to see it. About twenty minutes into the film, I looked to my left and noticed that Warhol had dozed off. Wait until he wakes up, I thought, am I ever going to give him shit.

I didn't have the opportunity. While Warhol catnapped through the first half of the film, I fell asleep during the second. As the movie ended and we were walking out of the building, we looked at each other. "Interesting movie, huh?" I said. "Oh, yeah," he responded. We stood on a street corner debating a trip downtown to a party. I said I was really too tired; if only the party had been in midtown. He agreed it was really too far, so we decided to call it a night.

"Boy, are we boring," I noted.

"God, we really are," he said.

When Warhol died at the age of fifty-eight on February 22, 1987, I was not alone in feeling stunned at the news. He hadn't been sick that I knew of, and he'd gone to such great lengths to stay healthy.

On April Fools' Day, a memorial mass was scheduled for St. Patrick's Cathedral. Calvin, Bianca, and Halston were among the mourners needing only one identifying name, as Warhol had needed only Andy. From Don Johnson to Philip Johnson, a strange collection of universes collided.

It wasn't as somber an event as expected, and many of the mourners laughed, or at least smiled, at the reading of some of Warhol's writings, including speculation as to how glamorous it would be to be "reincarnated as a big ring on Elizabeth Taylor's finger," and an analysis of the appeal of the Factory, which, he'd written, wasn't him: "I was the one hanging around everybody else . . . They came to see each other. They came to see who came."

All I knew about the original Factory was what I'd read in magazines, or in books like *Edie,* which painted an unfavorable portrait of Warhol as a voyeur who never lifted a helping hand, and probably encouraged Edie Sedgwick and other Factory hangers-on like her to the excesses that led to tragic and early ends. This was not the Warhol I knew, but I hadn't been around in those days. If he had ever been that calculatingly callous, he seemed to have changed by the time I met him.

According to art historian John Richardson, who spoke at the service, Warhol never fit that portrait in the first place. Richardson talked of Warhol's devotion to the Roman Catholic faith, his "secret piety" and of a misconception that Warhol encouraged the Factory groupies to self-destruct. "They were bent on destroying themselves," Richardson declared. "Nothing in the world was going to deter these lemmings from their fates."

After the service, there was, of course, a party, at a club on West Forty-sixth Street. I walked in and looked around the room. It was packed with faces, many of them famous, from the different worlds Warhol inhabited. It was an Olympic event.

Claus von Bülow was there. At St. Patrick's, he'd taken communion, leading to speculation about his having gone to confession. Another guest was Anne Bass, who'd lost her husband, Sid, of the Bass family fortune of Texas, to socialite Mercedes Kellogg in one of the season's more stunning stratagems. The world of fashion was represented at one end by the funk of Stephen Sprouse, and at the other by the haute chic of Carolina Herrera. Writers ran the gamut from Tama Janowitz, whose *Slaves of New York* had made her the darling of the downtown demimonde, to Dominick Dunne of *Vanity Fair,* a crafter of uptown prose.

It was as though players from every field had left their respective turfs and retreated to neutral ground—a club in midtown that hadn't officially opened yet, and therefore couldn't be misconstrued as belonging to one or another of the teams—to honor their favorite fan, the one who had held them all in equal esteem. To Warhol, they had all been "greeaaaat," even when the playing got rough, and they were temporarily tossed from competition, as Sprouse had been, financially, when his original design business failed, or as Bass had been, personally, when her husband deserted her.

By then, I was used to entering these sorts of celebrity arenas, and did so with increasingly less trepidation, in part due to a recurring and reassuring thought: perhaps Warhol would be there, and we could pace the sidelines together.

But he was gone, and with him went the indefinable mark he'd made on the games. His departure didn't end the play for anyone else.

The intensity of the maneuvers in social sports can lead to the impression that certain participants are key, and that the action must be halted if those participants are injured, or for some other reason pulled from play. That impression is an incorrect one. Every season there are new stars, some of whom line up with the old, while other rookies knock the more established from their positions.

It can get rough. It can get vicious.

You know, being hopelessly uncoordinated is not such a terrible condition.

Chapter 8

FRENZIED TRIO
STALKS DEEP DISH

Yes, there were lunches at the Four Seasons, nights at Studio 54, trips to Washington and California and, one spectacular weekend, several months after I took over Page Six, a five-day trip to France for a gathering of balloonists, and celebrities, at Malcolm Forbes's château in Balleroy.

And then there was the day-to-day process of putting together a gossip column. The following is a condensed account of a typical day at Page Six in early 1985, when I was the editor, Richard Johnson the column's reporter, and Ruth Hunter the assistant.

It's 8 A.M. and the elevator is broken in my apartment building, so the super takes me downstairs in the service car. On the way he mentions, with a big grin, that he's seen me on a cable TV show the day before.

Suddenly, I see a potential benefit in appearing on television. If the super thinks I'm a TV star, maybe finally he'll fix the recurring leak in the ceiling of my apartment.

Though both my predecessors as Page Six editor ended up combining column duties with regular TV appearances, I've not had much luck with sporadic experiences on the small screen. For one thing, it's practically impossible to fill an entire Page Six and have extra items left over for a television appearance. Also, I'm not enthusiastic about wearing three layers of makeup, and hair spray makes me sneeze. "Let's tease it," said one of the TV station hairdressers. "It'll give ya more height." Ignoring my protests, she did, and I taped the show looking like someone with a deep admiration for Annette Funicello and her distinctly personal style.

Despite the intriguing prospect of a leak-free apartment, I think I'll stick to flat hair, and print.

By nine I'm in the office, the first to arrive in the fourth-floor drama department. My starting time has gotten later as the months have gone by, and I no longer feel the need to be in extra early, but today I have a lunch in midtown —a long and complicated process due to the *Post*'s end-of-the-island location. That day's newspapers—*Times, News,* Washington *Post, Wall Street Journal*—are piled on top of the previous day's newspapers and mail. It is an impressive heap. Next to my computer terminal sit the remnants of a pastrami sandwich. Mustard splotches decorate the keyboard, the sign that the printers have been using my desk again for their nocturnal lunches.

Behind the desk is a shelf upon which perches a tower built of several weeks' worth of newspapers. The tower is beginning to lean to one side. If it topples, lives will be lost, mine first.

My eyelids already are beginning to droop. The city desk woke me up at 3 A.M. to ask if I knew where to find Dennis Stein, beau of Elizabeth Taylor. How would I know where Dennis Stein is? Though I'm acquainted with Stein, a show biz hanger-on and friend to Frank Sinatra and other Hollywood heavies, I don't keep day-to-day tabs on his activities. Because I'm the gossip columnist, however, there are those at the city desk who assume I have a list of all celebrity home numbers and daily schedules, and they have no qualms about calling me at odd hours. Once they were looking for Caroline Kennedy; another time, it was Joan Rivers. In all instances, they are incredulous when, at 2 or 3 or 4 A.M., I am not able to offer any insights into the whereabouts of specific notables.

The earth-shattering reason for the phone call? Stein and Taylor have broken off their engagement. The story is made to order for the New York tabloids: local boy (Stein is from Sheepshead Bay in Brooklyn) woos, and wins, Hollywood legend. Actually, no one in New York can believe Stein is even dating Taylor, let alone on the verge of marrying her. For years a familiar face at parties, restaurants and clubs, Stein is an urban court jester, given to staccato delivery of one-liners. I'm not sure precisely what he does for a living, but he definitely has a job working for Ronald Perelman, my former boss Claudia Cohen's mega-rich husband. I've run into Stein with the Perelmans several times. He's the one telling the jokes.

When the Perelmans were married, Stein was still dating Taylor, and he brought her to the wedding—which led to lots of preceremony apprehension about the possibility of the movie queen stealing the spotlight from the bride. Claudia doesn't like having her spotlight stolen.

The phone rings. It is the Tattler.

"I can't believe you're there this early."

"Then why did you call if you didn't think I'd be here?"

"I've been calling since eight. I have the most unbelievable story."

"What happened?"

"Well, I was at this dinner party on the East Side—I

151

called you from the party, but you weren't around—and you're not going to believe what happened."

"Yeah?"

"Do you believe how sick this is? My shrink is going to have a field day with this one."

The conversation goes on in this vein for some time. Eventually, the Tattler tattles. I'm uncertain as to why he's worked himself into such a state. His anecdote is amusing, but hardly worth the high blood pressure. A glance at the clock reveals the rapid disintegration of the morning.

"I've got to go. The other phone's ringing."

"Isn't it a great item? Are you going to use it?"

"It sure is. I'll let you know."

Never tell a source an item isn't all that terrific. Sources tend to take these things personally. Instead, blame it on the executive editor: "I wanted to run the story, but Roger Wood killed it." If sources have proven track records, why bruise egos if the mark for once is missed?

A copyboy comes through the office with a cart carrying copies of the latest edition of the *Post.*

First things first: who is today's Wingo celeb? The circulation-boosting game that appears in the *Post,* Wingo is accompanied by photos, sometimes of buxom bimbos in bikinis, but celebrities often pose for them as well. The *Post*'s biggest coup so far has been persuading Rudolph Nureyev to wield a Wingo card. That, they ran on the front page. Who would be next, we all wondered? Laurence Olivier? I. B. Singer?

Flipping through the other pages, I see Liz Smith has scooped us with a Barbra Streisand story. Liz, who is well wired, particularly in the entertainment world, is Page Six's most serious competition. We scoop her too, but many days I pick up the paper to see she has scooped us. I am not the only one who notices this. On days when Page Six loses out on a big story, editors from the city desk will stroll over to our corner of the drama room: "Trounced again, eh?"

Suzy's column, also in the *Daily News*, gets a cursory glance. Suzy has a virtual lock on news of high society, but high society is territory infrequently invaded by Page Six. We consider her competition only in certain areas of show business. There is one show biz press agent who is known to be Suzy's best Hollywood source. Though many of her stories involve society figures, and list each and every guest at society parties, Suzy does score the occasional big Hollywood scoop, presumably planted by this particular press agent, whose clients she plugs relentlessly. Today, she's filed an interminable list of socialities who've attended a party in Palm Beach. I've never heard of any of them. Suzy, whose real name is Aileen Mehle, is known for sprinkling her columns with comments like "It's the only way, really" and "Who else would tell you these things?" I hope no one else would because I'd hate to have to read this stuff in more than one place. Prolonged perusal of long lists of boldfaced names prompts severe eyestrain.

In the old days of hot type, I imagine, the printers must have loved Suzy. Since 90 percent of the names in her column are the same ones she's run the day before, and the day before, and the day before, all they'd have had to do was pick up the metal type from an old Suzy column and rerun it: Mica and Ahmet, Chessy and Bill, Sam and Judy, Jerry and Betsy, Nan and Tom, Nan and Jerry, and Alice. Can't forget Alice.

The other columnists in the *Post* are also must-reads, including Cindy Adams, wife of Joey Adams, the *Post*'s humor specialist. In his column, Strictly for Laughs, Joey, whose humor is of the Borscht Belt strain, regales with revelations like: "Martin is the Dean of drinkers. He says he drinks to pass the time—the last time he passed was 1998. He started when Henny was a Youngman."

Cindy replaced Earl Wilson as our first-person gossip columnist when Earl retired in 1983. She also quickly became something of a celebrity obituary specialist, writing those "I knew them when" pieces when celebrities kick the bucket. Cindy apparently knows everybody, and when there is a spate of celeb deaths, she logs a lot of overtime. The obits contain remarks like: "How do you put tears into a typewriter?"

Cindy is very outspoken. For a time, her greeting to me when we'd run into each other at parties was: "You're so young you make me sick! I have blouses older than you!"

The trademark expressions she scatters about her column are less rarefied than Suzy's: "Listen, what do you want from me?"

I also look over Page Six for mistakes. If typos and minor errors are caught early enough, they can be fixed for later editions.

The lead story, about a feud over party leadership between Governor Mario Cuomo and Joseph Crangle, former New York state Democratic chairman, is pretty good, as are a couple of the shorter items, including one on José Feliciano being dropped from consideration to do commercials for a disc company because he refused to wear sunglasses in the ads. Feliciano's spokesman said the singer "didn't want to stereotype the blind thing."

There isn't much left over in the computer bank from the day before, but it's still early.

The phone rings again. It is an outraged reader from Queens.

"You have made a very big mistake in your column."

"What would that be?"

"The story about Bing Crosby's youngest son, twenty-five-year-old Harry, getting married?"

"Yes?"

"Nathaniel is Bing's baby, not Harry."

"Really?"

"I don't see why you people don't check your facts. Everyone knows Harry is not the youngest."

"Well, thanks, I'll look into that."

Now I have to call the library to see if we have blown the ages of the Crosby kids. Corrections are not fun reading, though, on a dead day, a correction at least fills space.

Now three of the phone lines are ringing. I ignore them. If I sit there fielding calls I won't get anything done.

But what if it's a source? I watch the lights flash off and on. Shit. Should I pick one up?

"Hello?"

"You tramp, you woman of the pavements!"

"Hello, Harvey." It's press agent Harvey Mann, whose greeting is unmistakable.

"Where were you last night?" I was supposed to go to a party Harvey was organizing at a nightclub, but decided it would run too late and went home instead.

"Oh, I was too tired."

"Well, tramp, you should have been there. It was divine. Everyone was ripped to the tits."

"Hold on, there's another call."

I push the hold button and pick up the other flashing line. "Yes? Um, no, I don't think she's in yet." I can tell from the voice it's a flack.

"No. [Pause.] Just send down the press release. It's 210 South Street. [Pause.] It's really better just to send it. It's not a good idea to come down yourself. You never know when they're going to be in the office."

Press agents frequently suggest dropping by in person to deliver press releases. I have discouraged this practice since the time Radio City sent someone to hype their Christmas extravaganza. I felt something lurking behind my chair. When I hesitantly turned around to see what it was, there stood a dwarf in a red and green ensemble, topped off by a peaked cap—presumably a holiday elf. I didn't have a coronary, but came close.

I pick up Harvey's line again.

"It was a flack."

"One of my people!"

"She wanted to know if we wanted to cover a press conference for Jockey underwear."

"Studs in shorts?"

"I think they'll be wearing clothes, Harvey."

"Who cares then?"

"Listen, I should go. I have to make some phone calls."

"Oh, really, my beloved? Too busy for an old Jew? Well, I've got to go anyway. I'm having my nails wrapped."

It's ten and the drama room's occupants are starting to arrive, including the rest of the Page Six staff, Richard Johnson and Ruth Hunter. A few years older than I, in his early thirties, Richard is tall and blond and WASPy. Ruth is about the same age, and coincidentally, she too is tall, blond and WASPy. I'm also sort of blond. At the city desk, we're known as "Stalag Six."

Richard settles down at his desk, as he does most mornings, with the words, "Got a lot of overmatter, huh?"

I inform the perennial optimist that, no, we do not have a lot of overmatter. We have no overmatter, in fact, and we will have to dig up much material for tomorrow.

"Bummer," says Richard. "I'm kind of tired."

He doesn't look it, but Richard never does. If I have to go to a party at a disco or nightclub it takes me a couple of days to recover. Those sorts of events never seem to get started until midnight or later, and I don't have the energy to attend many of them. Richard somehow manages. Area, Danceteria, Régine's, Club A. He hits them all, and still manages to show up on time, and in a coherent state, the next day.

Richard's social circuiting has led him to make the acquaintance of many people with accents. The Eurotrash scene is at its peak. He is forever getting phone calls from people named Graziella, Massimo, Bettina and Jacques. These people are even more difficult to understand than the deli flacks.

Maybe something is happening in the city room. I head toward metropolitan editor Steve Dunleavy's desk and start flipping through spiked copy. Dunleavy's working style is best described as manic. A longtime associate of Rupert Murdoch's, Dunleavy is doggedly loyal to the press lord he refers to as "the Boss." One of his early jobs for the Murdoch press empire was authoring a column in the *Star* called "Steve Dunleavy: The Man They Call Mr. Blood & Guts." He is usually talking to at least four people at once in the office, plus a couple of others on different phone lines.

A rakish sort, with a mustache and a manner I've heard described as "very Adolphe Menjou," Dunleavy, it's said, would do anything for a "good yarn, mate." One legend has it that Dunleavy, during his days as a reporter in Australia, was competing with his father, a journalist for a rival newspaper, for the same story. Dunleavy, the legend goes, slashed the tires on his father's car to beat him to the scoop.

"So, what's going on, Steve?"

"Liz and Dennis Stein. You were some bloody help trying to find him last night."

"Well, he's hardly my best friend, and besides, it was three o'clock in the morning."

"He's hardly my best friend, and it was three o'clock in the morning," he imitates me in a whining falsetto. "Rubbish! A newspaper never sleeps! And now I suppose you're looking for stories."

"A little story or two would be nice."

"Grovel. Down on your knees!"

"Dream on. I don't grovel this early in the day. Not until after five."

"No groveling, my cherub, no stories."

Trips to the city desk don't always yield material, but there are occasions when a reporter with a tip for the column is reminded to pass it along by seeing one of the Page Six staff drop by.

Before the morning slips into an itemless afternoon, I make the daily calls, about eight to ten quick phone contacts with my bank of most reliable New York and Washington sources. Calls to Hollywood sources come later in the day. I also on a regular basis flip through my Rolodex and phone two or three people with whom I don't have daily contact, but with whom it's useful to keep in touch. Many of these calls brings responses like "Funny you called. I was thinking of you yesterday. I heard this great story . . ."

Today, I start with a political source who's just back from business at the White House.

"So, where are my Ron and Nancy stories?"

"Dull, it was unbelievably dull. I didn't meet with Reagan—just staff people."

"Shit. Nothing?"

"Well, I might have a Mike Deaver story later in the week, but you'll have to wait on it a couple of days. I was just down there and I don't want anybody to suspect it comes from me."

"Oh, dear. I hope we don't lose it."

"You won't lose it. Nobody else knows."

Two more calls result in similar responses. Then a publishing source calls with a possible item about a deal Cher supposedly has signed to write her autobiography. This source is occasionally accurate, but also has been known to botch names, dates and other essentials. Ruth will check out the tip and see if there is indeed a story to be had.

Fred Dicker, the *Post*'s Albany correspondent, calls. He says he'll have another Mario Cuomo story late in the week. Dicker is one of our more diligent staff sources. Frequently helpful with items detailing a twist in the fate of one politician or another, he also has a keen eye for the anecdotal. Like his story on an encounter in Albany between Edwina Sandys, granddaughter of Winston Churchill, and State Senator John Calandra, who hails from Da Bronx. Upon hearing Calandra was from the borough that houses the Bronx Zoo, Sandys suggested a meeting be arranged between a panda from that New York zoo and a panda from the London Zoo. Taken aback, Calandra responded in the accent indigenous to New York's northernmost borough: "Whaddaya think I am? A pimp?"

Joanne Wasserman, a reporter in the *Post*'s City Hall bureau, also phones in, with an item about union leader Victor Gotbaum, but she too says the story will have to wait until later in the week. I'm beginning to think we may have to run a blank page the next day, listing all the coming attractions: "Stay tuned for stories on . . ."

It's after 11 A.M.—time for the morning meeting.

"Richard?"

"Not much."

"What about that Richard Pryor story?" We have been attempting to track down a report that the comedian is about to get married again, to a nineteen-year-old.

"It's going to be impossible to check out."

"Well, make some calls anyway. It might turn into something. Is that it?"

"I've got a minor thing about Mickey Rooney staying with *Sugar Babies* for another year."

"Lame. Strictly Saturday overmatter." Less well read than the weekday columns, Saturday is the least desirable placement for a story. The ultimate insult to a proposed item is to dub it Saturday overmatter, or, even worse, potential Saturday overmatter. We never admit this to anyone from the outside, however. If someone pleads that an item run on any day but Saturday, we respond indignantly: "What's wrong with Saturday?"

"What do you want? It's early. Also, I'm should have the Richard Gere story today." Richard Gere is supposed to be replacing an ailing Burt Reynolds in a Sidney Lumet movie about political consultants.

Ruth runs through her list of possible items, and also dumps that day's mail on the desk, divided into two piles: "Possible" and "Shit." In the latter are all the general press releases, which are of no use to us for the most part, but I scan them just in case. The former contains letters, invitations, interesting releases and "exclusive" tips.

"One other thing," says Ruth.

"What?"

"It's a good thing you're sitting down. The Showtime Deli flack says a 200-pound, walking, talking, joke-telling robot will be serving lunch there Thursday. I told him we weren't interested, but he wouldn't take no."

"Gosh, I hate to pass on that kind of exclusive."

"I figured. Items aside, today's crucial question is: where's a trendy literary bar I can go to tonight? A friend of mine from California wants to go to one."

"Ruth, I thought you knew all the hip and trendy places."

"I guess not."

Richard suggests taking a six-pack to the library. Ruth is not amused.

It's time to start thinking about a lead story. Not having a lead makes me nervous. Today, I don't even have an idea for one. I call a journalist source.

"I'm desperate."

"So what else is new?"

"No, really, I need a lead."

"It's dead, dead, dead. Everybody's in Palm Beach. Don't you read Suzy?"

"Got another call. I'll call you back."

It's my Deaver source. He hasn't even given me the item, and he's already nervous.

"Don't mention anything to anybody about Deaver."

"Who am I going to tell?"

"I mean it. If you even say you'll have something on him in a couple of days, you could blow this."

"I won't say anything. I promise."

161

I hope it isn't another Deaver diet book story. After dropping thirty-five pounds, Deaver, White House deputy chief of staff, decided he'd pick up a few bucks by spilling his gut, so to speak, in a diet book. He said he needed the money, but White House ethics said he shouldn't capitalize on his government post while still holding that post. We've already done a couple of stories on the fate of the book, and I don't think it's time for another. Not that we've OD'd on diet stories.

From the time of Claudia Cohen on, Page Six has been very big on stories about weight, lost or gained. During the 1984 presidential race, we ran an entire series of stories on California Democrat Alan Cranston, who was doing the unthinkable—TRYING to gain weight. A jogger with a gaunt visage, Cranston felt his appearance would be enhanced by a few extra pounds, hence a high calorie diet, the course of which Page Six charted in great detail.

Cranston didn't do too well in the race, but he was tops in my candidate compendium. Not only did I get lots of copy out of his diet, but he also tinted his locks:

"Alan Cranston's hairdresser knew for sure. The problem was: so did everyone else, and that's why the presidential hopeful has stopped dyeing his hair."

A show biz source phones in a Madonna item. The Peroxided One has checked into a health spa in Mexico for some R&R. Actually, I can't remember if that's our trademark description for Madonna. After Page Six was the first to dub Michael Jackson "The Gloved One," we started attaching similar labels to other flamboyant celebrities. Boy George is The Mascaraed One. Or is it Prince? I get confused.

The source with whom I've scheduled a lunch calls to cancel, citing predictions of a blizzard.

Well, now at least there's more time to dig up material. On questionable days, I usually have an emergency lead, something that might not be worthy of the space at the top of the page, but, if nothing else turns up, can be expanded to fit the bill.

There are different kinds of emergency leads. Some are seasonal: Who's going where for the Fourth of July or Christmas? What will celebrities be using for New Year's Day hangover remedies? Others revolve around fashion: Who will wear what to the Tonys, or the Oscars? The only problem with seasonal stories is the possibility of colliding with another columnist equally hard up for material.

Books and magazines come in handy for back-up lead material. Eager to drum up reader interest, publishers send product early to Page Six and other columns. But we use books or magazines only if we are the lone column to have received the material in advance.

With little free time, I'd rather read a novel than *Debby Boone—So Far* but if Page Six had passed up that autobiographical page-turner, we would have missed the opportunity to reveal that Pat Boone spanked all four of his daughters well into their teen years, and that Debby, according to her publisher, came to realize "it was good for her."

Today's emergency back-up lead is a ballot for the annual Best-Dressed List, which has just gone out to fashion arbiters for this year's tabulations, accompanied by a "reference sheet" of those notables, including Diana Ross, Diane Sawyer and Raquel Welch, thought to be spiffy enough for inclusion. If I use it, the lead will be a list of names as long as one in a Suzy column, but I may have to if nothing else comes through.

The next call comes from a reader unhappy with the editorial content of the cartoon on top of Page Six. I explain that the *Post*'s cartoonist, Paul Rigby, operates independently of the gossip column, despite the fact that we share the space on the *Post*'s sixth page. I suggest he phone Rigby, or leave a message.

"Are you the editor of Page Six?" asks the reader. "Gimme a yes or no?"

"Yes."

"Then don't pass the buck, lady."

Oh well. I don't mind fielding a call for Rigby. It's the least I can do to thank him for introducing all of us to the fine points of the Limp Fall. Known for more than his talents with pen and ink, Rigby is the former world champion, and longtime world president, of the international organization of Limp Fallers.

The Limp Fall is an Australian sporting innovation entailing a fall to the floor of an establishment in which drinking is being done. It's difficult to describe the traits distinguishing a Limp Fall from an ordinary drop to the floor, but if you were to wander into a room of drunk Australians Limp Falling, you'd know you were seeing something special.

Opportunities to observe champion Limp Fallers in action is just one of the many perquisites that comes with employment at the *Post.*

The next time I pick up the phone, former Page Six editor Jim Brady is at the other end of the line.

"Dennis Stein and Liz are the talk of Sheepshead Bay." Brady grew up in the same Brooklyn neighborhood as Stein.

"So what's the word?"

"The ring."

"Yeah?"

"Everybody's saying: Dennis, you should have bought wholesale."

It's about one-thirty. We run through a progress report on items for the next day. The Cher book story has fallen through, Ruth reports. Richard says the Richard Gere story has checked out. With Gere, and Madonna, we have the two necessary picture items. We also have an item on City Council president Carol Bellamy, and one involving an actor from an off-Broadway show abandoning the stage for TV. The Best-Dressed List can serve as a double column—or a lead if nothing else appears—but that still leaves five or six holes to be filled.

There's no need to worry yet, though half the day is gone. There may be no activity in the way of incoming stories for the next three hours. On the other hand, three or four phone calls in the next fifteen minutes could set the whole column in place and we could be out of the office by five. There is never any way to tell—though we always speculate as to why certain times are busy and others are not.

If it's January, and slow, we say: "Everybody went to Florida." In July and August, we postulate: "Everybody's in the Hamptons." But then there are days in late August when the phone rings off the hook with great stories, and snowy winter days when an extraordinary influx of material has the column wrapped up by 4 P.M. Go figure.

Joe Rabinovich (a.k.a. Joe Rab), the features editor who nightly reviews our copy, hates it when I end an item with the remark "Go figure." He also hates "Stay tuned." And for a lead to an item, he loathes and detests "It's not easy being [fill in celebrity name]." That, he says, is a lazy way to start a story, as the others are lazy and overused ways to end stories.

Joe Rab also keeps a close watch for abuse of Yiddish expressions. He says he once counted seven *shleps* and four *kvetches* in a one-week period, which was, in his opinion, entirely too much Yiddish. I rationalized that certain items —particularly those involving New York delis—cry out for *kvetches* and *shleps*. He didn't agree. We can't seem to come to a meeting of the minds on this issue.

Ruth is signaling to me from her desk. She's on the phone, obviously recording the details of a very big story.

"Another C. Fred Bush exclusive."

C. Fred Bush, the canine companion to George Bush's family, is one of Page Six's favorite celebrities and the co-author, with Barbara Bush, of *C. Fred Bush: A Dog's Life.* Whenever possible, Page Six runs C. Fred's photo. Upon finishing the story, Ruth declares: "Tell Jimmy Breslin to forget it. The Pulitzer's in the bag with this one."

A phone call summons me to the city desk where I am informed that the Chicago *Sun-Times,* also owned by Rupert Murdoch, will be starting its own version of Page Six and that the two women who'll be writing the column are coming to New York to observe the Page Six operation. I feel like a visual aid in a social studies class.

How do I explain matzoh ball items? Do they have press agents like Harvey Mann in Chicago? Will they be able to relate to C. Fred Bush?

The hours are slipping by. It's after three, and we still don't have a lead. We also don't have a trendy literary bar for Ruth. Richard is in a bit of a quandry because he is supposed to attend a restaurant opening that night but he can't remember where the restaurant is. With the inches of snow piling up outside, I'm not certain any of us will be going anywhere.

Richard takes a call from a heavy breather, who unfortunately doesn't mutter a lead, just a few obscenities.

It's so slow, I may be reduced to a repeat of the stomach distress lead, composed on a particularly dark day in December of 1983, when, at 6 P.M., we still didn't have a lead story. What we had were two items. The first involved the acting Landers sisters, Audrey, of "Dallas" fame, and Judy, who'd been on "B.J. and the Bear."

The two siblings, along with their mother, were struck with such severe food poisoning on a flight from Paris to New York they had to check into a local hospital upon arrival. "It was murder," said the mother, after having her stomach pumped.

The second item focused upon one of Page Six's favorite celebrities, the outspoken Truman Capote.

He too had been struck by a stomach ailment, and was under observation and on a bland diet in a New York hospital.

I strung them together with this lead:

"It's hard to believe. The plum puddings and Christmas cookies haven't yet begun to make the holiday tables groan, and already we've heard of several cases of severe stomach distress in the metropolitan area."

"IT'S EARLY SEASON FOR HOLIDAY TUMMIES," was the headline on the frantically conceived story, which ran, rather appropriately, on December 8, the Feast of the Immaculate Conception.

I couldn't have run the two items separately anyway. The column, I'm constantly reminded, is supposed to be a collection of different types of stories. If I turn up a lead and a double both dealing with political figures, I know I'll be told: "Too much politics. Hold one." It's hard to remember this, however, on slow days, when any and all copy seems welcome. If I'd slipped both stomach stories into the column as separate items on the same day, the reaction from Roger Wood would have been: "Dear girl, I detect not one, but two digestive disorder stories in the column for tomorrow. Have we become the newsletter of internal medicine?"

It's not deadline hour yet, in any case—not that I've ever been sure precisely what that hour is. "Soon" or "As early as possible," is the most specific time I can get out of any of the editors.

I've only written up a couple of items, and haven't gone over anything Richard or Ruth has done.

My two or three cigarettes per hour escalate to chain-smoking level. Still no lead. Richard is working on a story about Howard Stein, the former owner of Xenon, filing for bankruptcy, but it's doubtful the legal papers will be available by deadline time. Ruth is also in the middle of a potential lead, involving a TV movie based on the saga of Geraldine Ferraro, but that too may take a couple of days to pin down.

A trip to the ladies' room seems to be in order. I may stumble across a lead on the way there. Two of the stalls are occupied; the other is out of order. As I'm waiting, I listen to a conversation between the two occupied stalls:

"I've got a date on Friday."

"Somebody from the dating service?"

"Yeah."

"Great. So how many is this?"

"I've gone out with four."

"How much does it cost?"

"The guy told me if I renewed it would be $200 for three months."

"How many dates is that?"

"Eighteen."

"D'ja have any repeats so far?"

"One wanted to, but I said forget it."

"So, no luck really, huh?"

I'm feeling the same way about sources. Lots of them out there—even more than eighteen—but have I lucked out with a lead story with any of them?

Back at my desk, I decide not to get frantic. Not just yet. But I can feel it coming. All it will take is one more flack attack.

I have another cigarette and watch the smoke settle into a cloud over my head, a cloud I hope will ward off flacks and draw in lead stories.

After flipping through the Rolodex, I call a publishing source I haven't talked to in a while. I'm stunned, and immediately renew my faith in miracles. It's another Fatima: the source unleashes a potential lead.

Patti Davis is at work on a novel with a character who is elected governor of California, then President of the United States. Sounds alarmingly like a *roman à clef* to me. I'm not able to get a number for Davis, but Celebrity Service locates that of her agent. He is reluctant to discuss the plot of the novel. Crown, the publisher, is more forthcoming. The agent is good for other needed information, including a progress report on Davis's acting career.

With the information about the book, and some background on thespian endeavors, we may have enough for a lead. I call the library to dig up the needed background.

It's past four. Actually, it's more like five. The clips arrive and I sit flipping through stories chronicling the life and times of Patti Davis Reagan.

Dunleavy comes in from the city desk, curious as to whether we have located a lead.

"Hate to disappoint you, Steve, but no groveling today. I found a lead."

"You'll be back begging tomorrow, old girl."

After writing up the double column, and running through Ruth's and Richard's stories, I begin to draw the layout, marking the length of each story according to the column inches that appear on the computer screen.

Writing headlines is not mandatory. If I can come up with appropriate ones, fine. If not, Joe Rab writes them. Occasionally, I'm inspired, but headlines are not my forte. For years, I rested on the laurels of a headline written to accompany a story about the boyfriends of the L.A. Rams cheerleaders, known as Ewes. The headline was "EWES' GUYS."

For the two picture items, I call the library to send photo files of Madonna and Richard Gere, an only semi-satisfactory mix. For the head shots used on the two picture items, I like to have figures from disparate worlds. If one photo is of a show biz personality, it's good to have someone from another sphere entirely for the second. Tab Hunter and Jeane Kirkpatrick would be an ideal combination. I do my best to avoid running similar photos, not wanting a repeat of the day I handed in pictures of Bill Cosby and Eddie Murphy and was told that two black comics were not the proper blend.

Looking through photo files is often the highlight of the day. If you call for photos of Diane Keaton, you can track her cultural, and style, history—from *Hair* to *Annie Hall* to *Reds*—and all the hairdos in between. I am stunned at the number of now normal-looking women who once sported beehives.

Richard Gere and Madonna have risen to celebrity too recently to have contributed much in the way of variety to their files. I pick out recent head shots and hand them in, along with the layout.

When the copy is turned in, it would be nice to leave the next day's column behind and move on to other things, but that is rarely possible. The stories have to be reviewed. If I rush out before that process is complete, I'm instructed to call in to answer last-minute questions. At the theater, I call at intermission. Out to dinner, I call between courses. Sometimes I forget to call until it's too late and the copy already has been sent to the composing room. On those nights, Joe Rab says dryly: "I presume this is a social call."

It's after seven when Ruth and Richard split. I'm supposed to go to a movie screening that night, but its starting time has come and gone.

The phones continue to ring. One line trembles with the lilting tones of Indian singer Asha Putli. She is hosting a party at Tucano, the Eurotrash restaurant adjoining Club A, the Eurotrash disco:

"Darleeng, you must come. All the reely beeg people will bee there. We never get to talk, we must talk."

Unable to recall ever meeting Asha Putli, I'm not sure why there is such a pressing need for us to talk, so I tell her that, unfortunately, I have leprosy and can no longer go to parties.

"Darleeng, I am so sorry. Is it serious?"

Jerry Lisker, *Post* executive sports editor, drops by for a visit. Jerry's visits always begin with two things. First, he bums a cigarette. Then he tells me he just got back from

171

Vegas, or is about to go to Vegas. Always on hand for the major prizefights, Lisker seems to spend an awful lot of time in Vegas.

Lisker is another student of the "I take shit from nobody" school. One day, when Jim Brady was editing Page Six, Lisker came storming into our office. "Know any good lawyers in Buffalo?" he asked Brady. "I'm gonna need one."

At a press conference at Madison Square Garden, hockey legend Phil Esposito, unhappy with a story about him by *Post* sportswriter Phil Mushnick, attempted to lift Mushnick off the ground by jamming his finger up Mushnick's nose. They were to meet again in Buffalo.

"I'm gonna let him have it," Lisker fumed. "I'll teach him to stick his finger up my reporter's nose."

Lisker sometimes drops off a sports-related item, but not today. He just wants a cigarette.

Now that it's too late for me to make the screening, I opt for a gallery opening to which a friend has invited me. I call the *Post*'s cab service, wait for a car number, then collect my things and exit the building.

The snow has stopped. Traffic on the street is light. South Street is tranquil at times like this, when it's cold and quiet, and the air is crisp. Across the street, the East River glistens, and off to the right, the lower Manhattan skyline sparkles. Nearby, less majestic structures nestle neatly under the sheltering swoop of the highway as it leads to the Brooklyn Bridge.

The cab pulls up. The driver knows Dunleavy. They all do. "You work for Steve Dunleavy? Whatta guy. Heh, heh. I picked him up the other night—4 A.M. it was. Those Australians, I'll tell ya, they're something else."

We head for Lafayette Street, near Astor Place, and an

art gallery. The small space, where paintings of shoes that look like animals are on display, is packed with celebrities, mostly of the oh-so-hip "Saturday Night Live" crowd—Lorne Michaels, Paul Simon, Penny Marshall. Mikhail Baryshnikov is also there, talking to an actress named Carole Mallory, whose chief claims to fame are a part in a movie called *Take This Job and Shove It* and numerous romantic encounters with famous men. Someone remarks that Mallory is supposedly writing a book about her sexual experiences: "Baryshnikov better watch it or he may be the next chapter." From what I can observe, he doesn't look much interested in literary history.

As usual, I know of everyone in the room, but I don't know anyone, really, and I stand staring at the shoe paintings wishing my friend would hurry up and arrive. He does. He is acquainted with most of the people in the room. "Don't you know anyone?" he asks.

"Nope." I respond.

"It is astonishing, how few people you know. How do you do your job?"

(Pause.)

"I make it all up."*

* A daily newspaper is just like life: nothing stays the same. Since early 1985, many of the individuals mentioned in this chapter have undergone career changes. Ruth Hunter is a free-lance journalist. Richard Johnson took over as Page Six editor when I quit. Steve Dunleavy and Jerry Lisker left the *Post* for Channel 5, the Rupert Murdoch-owned TV station in New York. Roger Wood is now the *Post*'s editor in chief. Suzy switched from the *Daily News* to the *Post*. Joanne Wasserman and Paul Rigby jumped from the *Post* to the *Daily News*. Andrew Stein, not Carol Bellamy, is currently City Council President. The Chicago *Sun-Times* is no longer owned by Rupert Murdoch. Sportswriter Ghil Mushnick has left the *Post*.

And C. Fred Bush, I am sorry to report, has moved on to that great kennel in the sky—where no man is a wimp, and all dogs are Republicans.

Chapter 9

TRASH AXED FROM SWIFTY'S BASH

Swifty Lazar is shorter than I am. He's maybe five-three, five-four tops. I'm five-seven. When Lazar attempted to throw me out of his Academy Awards party, however, he suddenly seemed about six-five. I felt about four-three.

Of course, it might have been the reflection from his glasses, which are large, thick and black-rimmed, rather in the style of Mr. Magoo. When he's irritated, his spectacles illuminate a threatening and ominous glare. The thought of an undesirable crashing his party definitely irritates him.

In the world of deal-making, eighty-one-year-old Irving (a.k.a. Swifty) Lazar is something of a legend. At one time or another, agent and/or friend to such notables as Ira Gershwin, Cole Porter, Art Buchwald, Humphrey Bogart, Noel Coward and Richard Nixon, Lazar is a character even the most creative of his clients would have had a tough time inventing. They all talk about him as though they had.

Everyone who knows him has a Swifty story, and has heard a dozen more. Like an irritated agent, these tales have been known to grow mysteriously taller.

The one involving his nickname is fairly well documented. Humphrey Bogart dubbed him Swifty after the agent lined up five deals for the actor in a twenty-four-hour period. Lazar claims to be less than fond of the sobriquet and says, "Only people who know me very well—or don't know me at all—call me that."

There are the stories of his lack of interest in the printed word, except to sell it. Alan Jay Lerner supposedly sent him a copy of *An American in Paris* with all the pages taped together to test his reading habits. Lazar called him a few days later, made no mention of the tape and proclaimed it a "rare work of art."

The tales of Lazar's fastidiousness are many: he loathes the feel of a bare floor under his feet; he washes his hands constantly; he has his own linen stocked in his favorite hotels; he frequently carries disinfectant.

I have a few Swifty stories of my own, including one that doesn't involve a deal or dirt, but a party. The Party.

The agent is also known as a host, with the Academy Awards party he and his wife Mary throw each year the best known of his social accomplishments.

In the more than twenty years since its inception, the Lazars' Academy Awards party has become such a major Hollywood event that in 1978, when Oscar marked its fiftieth year, the producers of the awards telecast asked Lazar to skip a year, for fear his party would draw attention from the official anniversary gala.

But unless you're a Marvin Davis or a Liz Taylor or a William Hurt, an invitation is not automatic.

I began slipping my foot in the door more than a year before I actually attended.

It was 1983, soon after I became editor of Page Six. I didn't know Lazar very well, having until then only communicated with him by phone, and hadn't even begun to figure out a subtle way to invite myself to his Oscar party, when an opportunity presented itself.

After speaking to Lazar about a story involving one of his book deals, I suggested getting together in person. We arranged a date for lunch.

As he came to the door of his East Side apartment, where he'd instructed me to meet him, I realized that the countless pictures I'd seen of him on society pages did not convey a genuine image of Lazar in the flesh, a cue-balled gnome overwhelmed by enormous spectacles. His appearance matched his fastidious reputation. Every button was buttoned, every seam was straight. Had he any hairs, they'd all have been in place.

Le Cirque, the restaurant he'd chosen, was right down the street from his apartment.

"I always sit here," he said, pointing to a choice corner. I wasn't that ignorant. I knew a Good Table when parked at one.

Lazar seemed disappointed as he surveyed the packed restaurant. "No one's here," he commented.

He told me what to order. He told me how he worked: "When I say off-the-record, I mean it."

Part of the time, Lazar talks like a tough from some Damon Runyon-esque locale. At other times, his diction is marked by British inflections. For instance, he pronounces "dear" as "dee-ah," as in "my dee-ah." He's obviously spent a good deal of time with people whose high chairs regularly rest before Good Tables. I found it amusing that someone whose profession demanded fast talking and swift dealing could be so stiff when he chose to be. Once, when I asked him what he thought of the possibility of a book by the Mayflower Madam, Sydney Biddle Barrows,

Lazar promptly replied: "It's a sordid thing. I wouldn't handle it."

Eventually, I steered the luncheon chat around to the Oscar party, even though I was aware that he and his wife were not hosting one that year. Instead, they were planning a bash in New York at around the same time, following the opening of *Porgy and Bess* at Radio City Music Hall.

But there was always 1984.

"If you're in L.A. next year," said Lazar, "call us."

The months rolled by. I didn't see Lazar again, but I spoke to him several times on the phone. Suddenly, the Oscars loomed. Would he and Mary be having the party again, I asked?

"We're back by popular demand," Lazar declared. "People are panting in the streets to be invited."

Controlling my breathing, I mentioned that I was arranging a trip to the West Coast to cover the Oscars.

In truth, I hadn't even made hotel reservations or sought credentials to the ceremony. First, I wanted to see if I would be able to attend Lazar's party.

"You'll be going to the awards?" he asked. "Good. Come to us after."

There are actually two Lazar Oscar parties. The first is a sit-down dinner for approximately two hundred of the Hollywood elite. It draws such studio powers as Barry Diller and Alan Ladd, Jr., and a veritable galaxy of stars, from Joan Collins to Jimmy Stewart. During this part of the evening, table-hopping is not encouraged. Lazar rules the proceedings with an iron fist. You may be the head of Universal, but at Lazar's party you're just another guest, and if you should decide to switch seats in the middle of the show, you'll hear about it. "Sit down!" is his battle cry during that part of the party. If a movie were to be made about the event, it would have to be entitled *The Little Dictator.*

After the awards, which are viewed by the dinner guests on one of several TV screens placed at strategic points around the restaurant where the party is being held, a portion of the early group of revelers drifts out. Then the table-hopping begins, as the second shift, those who've participated in the program at the Dorothy Chandler Pavilion as presenters, nominees, winners or observers, comes trooping in. At the later, more casual, affair, it's easier to accommodate "drop-ins" like me.

"You'll see everybody after," Lazar promised. "If you miss anybody, I'll tell you."

Once I got to California and settled into my room at the Beverly Hills Hotel, I called a few studio contacts, then went down to the pool and looked around, noting a few familiar faces from New York as I did. This was my kind of assignment.

All I had to do was sit in a lounge chair and watch the items float in. Just by observing who was around the pool, I whipped up a "hanging out during Oscar weekend" story. People I knew sat down to say hello, leaving stories in their wake, including one about Eddie Murphy replacing Sylvester Stallone in a Paramount film called *Beverly Hills Cop.*

After a day or two at the hotel, I felt like an old hand. I still wasn't sure to whom I was supposed to slip money to get a good table in the Polo Lounge, but other than that I was getting the hang of things. Everything was going quite smoothly as Oscar day, Monday, arrived. I would be driving to the Dorothy Chandler Pavilion for the awards late that afternoon. After the ceremony, I'd arranged to go to Morton's, where another Academy Awards party was to be held, to pick up the friend who'd accompany me to a restaurant called the Bistro for the Lazar affair.

I made the error of requesting a seat in the audience to watch the show, rather than credentials to cover it from backstage. My seat was in nosebleed territory, and I couldn't see much of what was happening on stage. The show was interminably long, nearly four hours, and I was relieved to escape when it was over.

Wading through the traffic outside the auditorium seemed to take hours.

It must have taken hours. By the time I got to Morton's, that party was breaking up. All the guests were thoroughly blotto and my friend, according to the bartender, had grown tired of waiting and had left moments before I'd arrived.

I should have seen this as an omen. Proceeding to the Bistro in Beverly Hills, I left my friend's name at the door, just in case he was on his way there.

Slipping through the paparazzi at the entrance to the party, I looked for the host.

Lazar greeted me with open arms: "We're so glad you could come. Where's your date? We had you down for two."

I explained the Morton's mishap.

"Don't worry," Lazar assured me. "If you left his name, they'll let him in when he gets here."

"Everybody was here," he declared, running through a list of the Hollywood royalty who'd already left.

"Everybody is here," he added, pointing out a few of the crowned heads scattered around the room.

"Everybody will be here," he continued, listing the names of nominees and winners who'd be arriving in due course. Moments later, *Terms of Endearment* stars Shirley

MacLaine and Debra Winger walked in, followed by the film's director, Jim Brooks.

Lazar escorted me from the party's anteroom into a larger inner sanctum, away from the popping flashbulbs. He then scurried back to his front-door duties.

Jackie Collins, Jack Lemmon, Michael Caine and Andy Williams were among those I remember seeing. I spoke to Arnold Schwarzenegger, whom I'd met several days earlier during a visit to the set of *The Terminator*. He didn't remember me. I should have seen this as an omen.

I wandered back into the front room, avoiding a stop at the bar as I walked by it. When working on an empty stomach, I had discovered, it's best to avoid drinking. Ending up with your face in an ashtray is socially unacceptable in New York, and I presumed Hollywood as well.

Spotting someone familiar, Stephen Schiff, *Vanity Fair*'s movie critic, on the opposite side of the room, I headed in his direction, running right into Lazar en route.

"Are you alone, my dear?" he asked politely.

"Yes," I answered. "I told you what happened at Morton's, didn't I?"

"You mean you're not with anyone?" he inquired, raising his voice a notch.

"No."

"Then you'll have to leave," he declared definitively.

What a card that Swifty is, I thought, remarking aloud, "Very funny, Irving."

He didn't think it was.

"You will have to leave right now," he said, in a tone crackling with menace.

"You're kidding, right?"

"I most certainly am not," he said. "You are not wanted

here." He wasn't kidding, and he was beginning to look really, really mean, like a pit bull ready to pounce.

I didn't understand what was going on. Why would he greet me warmly one minute, then throw me out on my ear the next? I felt slightly out of place at the party, not the first time I'd experienced that sensation, but it never before had led to my ouster from an event. A chill went down my spine. As far as I knew, it was neither a sin, nor a crime, to attend an Oscar party without a date.

"I don't get it," I said nervously.

"You will very soon if you don't get out of here. Go—NOW—before I call someone.

He looked toward a couple of the large gentlemen lurking around the door. I pictured the *Post* headline: "COLUMNIST SLUGGED SENSELESS" and, in smaller type, "Replacement Sought."

"I really don't understand this," I said, reintroducing myself.

I won't say he jumped, but he did lurch back a bit, his brows raising above the rims of his glasses.

"Well, my dee-ah. I didn't recognize you!" he said, turning rapidly to his left, where Alan Ladd, Jr., while waiting to greet the host of the party, had witnessed the near-ejection.

"Alan, I want you to meet my best friend."

"Former best friend," Ladd corrected.

"Her hair's different," Lazar explained. From ten minutes earlier?

He took me by the arm and dragged me to the back room, where he proceeded to introduce me to everyone in sight. "You must know Jack Lemmon. This is Johnny Carson. Have you met Jennifer Beals?"

Before taking off for the front door once again, Lazar

left me with actor Roger Moore and producer Elliott Kastner. "You must come to the house tomorrow for drinks," he said. "I'll call you at the hotel."

Still in a somewhat dazed state, I nodded. Moore and Kastner were exchanging witticisms.

"Elliott, what happened to that picture we talked about? You know, the one you offered Sean Connery and Michael Caine and Sammy Davis."

"Have you dreamt about me lately, Roger?" asked Kastner.

"No," said the actor. "Lately my dreams have been very dry."

"Well, I had a dream about you," the producer continued.

"Really?" asked Moore, in his most urbane "007" manner. "I hope I was on top because my hemorrhoids are killing me."

Not feeling up to this sort of joking, I glanced back at the door. Michael Jackson had just walked in, to an enthusiastic greeting from Lazar, who didn't need to be reminded who Jackson was. It had to be the sequins. I knew I should have worn something glitzier, and if I ever had to cover this party again, I would aim at flashier attire. Maybe a tasteful tiara.

Passing by the bar again, I gave in and ordered a drink. Stephen Schiff, who'd caught the final moments of my almost-ouster, walked over. "What was that all about?" he asked. "I thought the ax was going to fall on me next. I thought maybe he'd decided to throw out all journalists."

"It's not easy being a byline," I commented.

My drink downed, I looked for the ladies' room. As I opened the door, a startled Liza Minnelli said, "Oops! I didn't think anyone else would come in or I wouldn't have invited my friend."

Her friend—sequined glove and all—disappeared into one stall. Was I supposed to leave? Forget it. It was, after all, the ladies' room. I had more right to be there than Michael Jackson. I entered the other stall.

When I emerged, Minnelli was talking on the boudoir phone. "Dad," she whispered. "I'm here with my friend Michael."

As I approached the sink, they began a duet of "They Call the Wind Mariah" into the receiver.

"This sure is a bizarre party," I noted to a fellow journalist as I exited.

"Where's Michael Jackson?" she asked. "Isn't Michael Jackson supposed to be here?"

"He's in the ladies' room."

"Oh."

I went to find another phone to call the office in New York. When I returned, Jackson and Minnelli were standing in the hall outside the entrance to the party, where Jackson was signing an autograph for one of the waiters. Until that evening, I had never asked anyone for an autograph, and probably never will again, but at that point, I figured, what the hell? With my Academy Awards program in my hand, I approached. Jackson signed it quickly, without looking up.

Back in the party, the crowd from *Terms of Endearment*, including Jim Brooks, winner of the three Oscars that night as the movie's writer/director/producer, was accepting congratulations. After telling him how I'd run into Michael Jackson in the ladies' room and had requested my first autograph, I asked if he wanted to be the second.

Before signing his name on the program I handed him, Brooks wrote: "To a strange autograph hound."

Moments later, Joan Collins tackled Michael Caine trying to get to Michael Jackson. Would violence follow? It seemed time to split. I bid Lazar farewell. "I'll call you tomorrow about drinks," he called out as I exited. It was three-fifteen by the time I got back to the hotel.

The next morning, after filing my Oscar stories over the phone to New York, I went down to the pool to pass out in the sun. Just as I'd sunk my head into a lounge chair, I was paged by the hotel operator.

"Hello, my dear. Did you enjoy the party? Did you get all the names?" Lazar ran through a list of all the late arrivals, in case I'd missed one or two. After giving me directions to his home, and the time I should drop by that afternoon, he ended the phone call with a warning:

"Only come if you're writing a nice story. Not if you're one of those reporters who comes west and writes bad things about Hollywood. I don't like that kind of reporter."

First the guy tries to throw me out of his party, and now he's dictating story content. I contemplated telling him what he could do with his invitation for drinks, but I was certain I'd get a good story out of it. When it comes to a story, I often surprise myself with my willingness to ignore insults, and their possible ignominious consequences.

Lazar's home is so high in the hills, my ears popped en route. "Come in," Lazar greeted me. "I'm on the phone. I'll just be a minute."

As I stood in the front room, adrift in a sea of floral arrangements, bits of conversation drifted in from the next room: "Did you see Michael Jackson?"

When Lazar returned, I admired the flowers, in particu-

184

lar a large arrangement that resembled a miniature Japanese garden. He sighed: "All from guests. There are too many. Everyone thinks they have to send something, so they send flowers. We've got to get rid of them, give them to the neighbors or something."

Before beginning the interview, Lazar gave me a tour of his home, starting with a painting in the front room.

Though my command of art history pretty much begins and ends with the "Mona Lisa," I assumed the painting— of a naked woman holding a hat—was an original by some modern master. But when Lazar said, "That's my mother," I wasn't quite sure. It's hard to tell when he's kidding. "Really?" I commented.

"Ha, ha. That's very funny." It was indeed by some famous painter, though I can't remember which one. From then on, he identified the artist: "That's a Picasso. Here's a Degas."

Finally, we sat down for the interview, which I knew wouldn't be easy. Lazar is well acquainted with the rules of the game and prefaces his most interesting remarks with "This is off-the-record."

"So, how do you plan the party?"

Lazar settled himself.

"People don't know what it is to plan this. We only have really class people. No trash. Kirk Kerkorian was supposed to come, but was ill. His girl came, Yvette Mimieux. She wanted to sit with a woman friend, so we changed her from Cary Grant's table to a terrible table. But she wanted it. Then she said 'This is a terrible table. I want to move back to Cary Grant's.' But Mary had to tell her we can't do that kind of thing. There are too many details to work out."

As Lazar continued, he was interrupted several times by

the phone, each call regarding the events of the night before. He related several examples of less-than-acceptable behavior on the part of guests who'd never again fall into that category at one of his parties. All of these examples were preceded by "This is off-the-record. Don't print it." I said I wouldn't.

Lazar moved onto other topics, like politics ("I'd never vote for Ted Kennedy. He's a coward.") and music ("The Beatles were geniuses, but this hard rock stuff, I can't stomach it.")

Mary Lazar arrived home from work at her film production offices. "Wasn't the party fun?" she said. "I turn into a groupie when I see Michael Jackson. I held his glove."

Her husband admired her new jeans. His wife reminded him of a dinner engagement. I looked at my watch and coughed: "My, it's gotten so late. I should be going."

"We're so glad you could come," said Lazar, leading me to the door. He always seemed to be leading me to a door. "Call us if you need anything. Anything at all."

I couldn't think of anything and made no requests for the remainder of my stay in California, or during the next several months—except for the occasional quote for an article in the *Post*.

The Oscars reared their heads again. I'd certainly gathered more interesting material at the Lazar party than I had at the ceremony itself. Maybe I'd skip it this time, and try and attend the entire Lazar affair.

Recalling the events of the year before, I anticipated no problem gaining admittance. After what had happened, how could he refuse me?

Like this: "I don't know. We've got too many people as it is. Call me in a couple of weeks."

Here's the thing about Swifty Lazar and his Oscar

party: he is under the impression that it is the most important social gathering of the year in a town where social
gatherings play a very important role. It's a correct impression in some respects, in that it does fall into the category of a "hot ticket." But really, he does tend to get a bit
carried away. A party, after all, is only a party. In this
case, however, it's his party, and a private one. Not a formal press event, though it garners more ink than any official Oscar party, Lazar's party is off-limits to anyone not
up to the host's standards.

But for someone like me, the Lazar party is an important one to attend. Even so, I almost dropped the idea at
his first sign of hesitation. I'd only sink so far in the quest
of a good story. Groveling before someone who'd very
nearly planted a foot in my posterior and shoved me in
the direction of the stairs the year before was a step too
low.

Still a little obsequiousness wouldn't kill me, so, before
discarding my plans, I tried again.

"It doesn't look good. Call back later."

That did it. He could have his stupid party. I'd cover the
awards from backstage and leave it at that. Then, he called
me.

"We fit you in. I've got you at a good table."

What was a Good Table as far as I was concerned? Cary
Grant, or off in a corner with Yvette and the girls?

The recognition factor didn't turn out to be a problem
that year. Lazar invited me over to his house for drinks a
couple of days before the party. The afternoon of the Oscars, I leisurely prepared to drive to Spago, the trendy
Hollywood eatery owned by Wolfgang Puck, and the site
of the 1985 party.

Officially, the Lazars said they shifted the party from

the Bistro to Spago for simple want of a change. The rumor mill in Hollywood said the switch was engineered for other reasons—perhaps because Lazar feared a rival party at Spago, which had stolen some of his thunder the year before, might eclipse his in star power. Particularly young star power. Though Lazar's party drew much of Hollywood's old guard, it wasn't as hot an attraction as it had once been with new screen faces.

Whatever the reasons, it proved a successful move. The stars collected at Lazar's in 1985 made Oscar '84 look lackluster in comparison. Marvin Davis, Barry Diller and other studio heads mingled with on-screen names like Jacqueline Bisset and Gregory Peck. For media mavens, cheap thrills were apparent in the presence of Walter Cronkite and Mike Wallace.

There were but two or three reporters admitted to the first part of the party. Barbara Howar of "Entertainment Tonight" was the only one accompanied by a TV crew. Though Lazar had approved her bringing in cameras, he kept trying to move her along. As she approached the table where Johnny Carson was seated with several women, including his then girlfriend Alexis Maas, Lazar barked, "Get that out of here! He doesn't want any cameras."

Carson, with his arms around two of the women, smiled for the "ET" crew and didn't look as though he abhorred the attention at all.

Before the broadcast actually started, and I was locked to my seat, I wandered back to Andy Warhol's table. In California to film a guest spot on "Love Boat," Warhol said his favorite thing about the TV experience so far was the peanut butter and jelly served on the set. Being a bit player appealed to him, he said. He liked the existence of "an invisible person."

When the program began, I returned to the Good Table where I'd been placed, to watch the show lumber on in traditionally ponderous fashion. Jack Haley, Jr., a former producer of the Academy Awards broadcast, had been describing the nearly impossible task of keeping the show to a reasonable length, when Laurence Olivier, in announcing *Amadeus* as Best Film, neglected to name the other nominated pictures. Someone called out: "Hey, Jack, if you'd had Olivier when you were doing the show, you could have cut it by fifteen minutes."

Raquel Welch, at the same table, commented: "Do you think he really did it on purpose to save time? I figured he probably just forgot to read the other ones."

There was a moment of silent disbelief at our table, which I broke by telling Welch her dress was just lovely and asking her who'd designed it.

Motown executive Suzanne de Passe took a call from Diana Ross, who was phoning from backstage at the awards. She yelled to Lazar: "Swifty, is it all right if Diana brings Tom Selleck?"

I expected Lazar to respond: "No! I didn't invite him," but, obviously feeling magnanimous, he said, "Sure she can."

Once the awards were over, the second shift began drifting in from the ceremonies. Jimmy Stewart, Cary Grant, Gene Kelly, Candice Bergen, Sissy Spacek, Whoopi Goldberg, Sally Field and Stevie Wonder were among the post-Oscar arrivals.

Every time I approached the unisex bathrooms, there was a line: Farrah Fawcett and Alana Hamilton one time; Laurence Olivier the next.

As the area near the door became more congested, Lazar appeared more and more agitated. I related my experience of the year before to a producer standing next to me.

"That's nothing," he said. "He's tried to throw me out twice tonight. Stay away from the door. When it gets this late and this crowded, he starts throwing everybody out."

Looking at my watch, I realized it was time to find a phone and dictate a late story to the *Post*'s city desk in New York. A bartender directed me to an empty office on the second floor.

As I started to read my hurriedly composed "Stars Glitter at Swifty's Oscar Bash" story, the door to the office opened and Farrah Fawcett walked in. She picked up a phone on the other side of the room and started crying. Right before I'd come upstairs, I'd seen her proudly passing around photos of her and Ryan O'Neal's then four-month-old son, Redmond. I had no idea what had transpired in the ensuing minutes, but it obviously hadn't been pleasant.

The dictationist I was talking to in New York asked: "Is that somebody crying?"

"Uh, no," I said. "It's a cat."

Another woman came into the office and started patting Fawcett on the shoulder. As I only had about five minutes to finish the story, I didn't feel like leaping across the room with my notebook and asking, "Why are you crying? Tell me quick so I can fit it into my story," although metropolitan editor Steve Dunleavy would have expected no less of me, I'm sure.

Dunleavy had another assignment for me, in any case. He took the phone from the dictationist: "Where does this F. Murray Abraham [who'd earlier in the evening been named Best Actor for his performance in *Amadeus]* live in Brooklyn? You got a number or address for him?"

I told Dunleavy that F. Murray and I had never been close.

"Well, you're at a fucking Hollywood party. Go get it! Somebody there has to have it!"

I wondered whom to ask of the celebrities I'd seen downstairs? Maybe Linda Evans and Abraham were old pals? Alan King? Dinah Shore? Somehow, Abraham didn't strike me as a Spago kind of a guy.

I returned to the party. Lazar was in an ebullient mood: "Are you having a good time, doll? Let's get you a drink."

Scanning the crowd, I realized that Lazar's oft-repeated "Everybody is here" was only partially correct. The crowd from *Amadeus,* the evening's big winners with eight Oscars, was nowhere to be seen.

Their absence went unnoticed. Lazar was beaming. His wife Mary was beaming. Wolfgang Puck was beaming as he watched Gene Kelly perch on the stairs to eat one of his pizzas.

I wasn't beaming. I had no idea how I'd get F. Murray Abraham's number. About the only person in the room who might even know Abraham was another New York actor, William Hurt. The thought of going up to Hurt and saying, "Yo, Bill. You got F. Murray's number on you?" was not too enticing.

Lazar certainly wouldn't have it, though his address book undoubtedly was replete with unlisted celebrity numbers.

A couple of days before, Lazar had said to me: "We don't invite everybody to the party. It's impossible."

As far as nominees were concerned, he'd said: "I only

invite those I know and like. I don't know this Abraham so I didn't invite him."

The *Post* went to bed that night without my aid in the F. Murray Abraham home phone number department.

Two years later, I went again to the Lazar Oscar party, this time after covering the awards from backstage.

Rupert Murdoch was walking out the door as I approached it. Inside the restaurant, seats at the best of the Good Tables were occupied by Elizabeth Taylor, Joan Collins, Lauren Bacall, and John Huston. As the evening wore on, people like Christopher Reeve, Bette Midler, Sigourney Weaver, Kathleen Turner and Dustin Hoffman drifted in.

More reporters than usual had been admitted, and I felt less obtrusive asking people for quotes, but, frankly, I was overwhelmed. I sat down at a table near the back of the eatery.

A waiter placed a plate of desserts on the table. As I was contemplating trying one, Shirley MacLaine walked by. She looked at the desserts, picked up one and took a bite, then returned it to the plate. She picked up another and did the same thing, then another. On her fourth try, she seemed satisfied and walked away with her final selection.

Talk about undignified dessert consumption.

I felt as one might when presented with a box of chocolates which, from an aerial view, looks relatively untouched, but upon further examination, all the caramels and nuts have been removed and those remaining are the less desirable cream-filled, with holes punctured in the bottom by some earlier explorer.

Another journalist had joined me: "Is that Joan Collins? I can't believe that's Joan Collins. I didn't think she was a real person."

I wasn't sure any of them were real people, least of all Joan Collins, who resembled a figure in a wax museum. Lazar, who that year celebrated his eightieth birthday, looked more surreal than most as he maintained his post at the door, welcoming celebrity after celebrity after celebrity.

As one after another entered, pumped Lazar's hand or kissed his cheek, moved in and began socializing, I felt as though I were watching product being spewed forth from a celebrity assembly line. At some point that night, I envisioned a component in each malfunctioning, effectively ending the party.

It may have happened eventually. I don't know. At about one-thirty, I walked out of the restaurant. Crowds of stargazers were pressed against barricades waiting for a glimpse of the famous guests.

The first time I attended Lazar's party, I might have ended up on the other side of the barrier, had he been successful in throwing me out. Though he hadn't, I still felt like a crasher. At these kinds of parties, all journalists, even the invited ones, are crashers, because, really, wouldn't the celebrities have a better time if no one was there taking notes?

Maybe not. They'd probably have no desire to go if they hadn't read Lazar's party described umpteen times as "The hottest bash in Hollywood."

Just then I ran into a reporter I knew from New York, who hadn't been able to break through the gates.

"My name's supposed to be on the list, but it's not," she lamented. "Is it still worth trying to get in?"

"Not if you want dessert," I said.

193

Chapter 10

LIZ STORMS
NORMANDY BEACHES

While sipping an espresso in the lobby of the Hotel Royal in Deauville, I chatted with an editor and a photographer from Fleet Street, who, like me, had traveled to the seaside resort northwest of Paris to cover the annual American film festival.

The Brits were relieved that Elizabeth Taylor finally had exited. Her presence at the 1985 festival had attracted an inordinate number of amateur photographers and film groupies, making it difficult for professionals with deadlines to gather material.

Just then, one of the hotel's doormen ran through the lobby: *"Elle est de retour!* Leez eez back!"

"My god, that woman's like a bad penny," said the Fleet Street photographer, grabbing his camera bag and bolting up and out through the hotel's revolving front doors, which faced the ocean, and, before the sand and sea, a large grassy area where only minutes before Liz Taylor had taken off in a helicopter bound for Paris.

She had been late in taking off and now she was back. Taylor didn't do anything according to schedule. She hadn't done anything according to schedule all week.

Taylor, who'd been honored with a film retrospective at the festival, had been rushing to Paris where she would be given an arts award by the French government. The other Englishman and I walked out to see what had happened.

Not a light traveler, Taylor had more suitcases than the helicopter could accommodate. She took only one or two with her, sending the rest in a car that would follow to Paris. Once the copter had whirled off, she discovered that the dress she planned to wear at the awards ceremony in Paris was missing, and therefore must have been placed in one of the valises in the car. She instructed the pilot to return to Deauville, where the chopper rested on the lawn opposite the Royal until another car, sent speeding out of town to capture the first, retrieved the dress and brought it back to Taylor, who was obviously possessed of a keen sense of priority.

The return of Taylor brought a return of her groupies, including one frightening Frenchman reminiscent of fans like Mark David Chapman and John Hinckley.

His gangly frame was crowned with a head seemingly too large to remain balanced, and above his long pointed nose rested a pair of dark pinholes that widened at the sight of Taylor. Burdened with two or three cameras and extra lenses, he would dart off in the direction of the actress, pulled to one side, then the other, by the swinging equipment, all the while bleating "Leeeez! Leeeeez!" in a tone similar to an animal's on the verge of slaughter. After one hotel exit by Taylor, I heard him hysterically exclaiming to an American photographer: *"Mon dieu!* I say 'Leez' and she look at me! She like me. I know she like me!"

Had I been in Liz Taylor's shoes, I never would have left my hotel room, knowing that every appearance would bring forth a rush of fans eagerly intent on Taylor worship.

She didn't leave her quarters very often. My room was right down the hall from what had been redecorated and redubbed "Suite Elisabeth Taylor" in her honor. I saw little of her, though her hairdresser, Monsieur Alexandre, was very much in evidence, usually wielding a teasing comb or some other implement of the tress trade.

Hair, nails and makeup were key ingredients of the festival that year. When Taylor arrived in Paris en route to Deauville, she made the private plane sit on the runway for an hour until Monsieur Alexandre and his combs arrived. As soon as she hit Deauville, she announced that a nail had been broken and had to be repaired *toute de suite* in the privacy of her suite.

It was a good thing she decided to spend her first day resting. If she'd emerged on schedule, she would have collided with Debbie Reynolds, another American being honored that year, and also a fellow ex-Mrs. Eddie Fisher.

Festival organizers had timed the visits by the two actresses to avoid such a confrontation, but Reynolds, also staying at the Royal, threw things off kilter when she decided to stick around beyond her scheduled hour of departure.

Accompanied not only by her hairdresser, but by her hairdresser's sister as well, Reynolds, whose sturdy coiffure resembled a blond helmet, was having such a lovely time she lingered, Liz be damned.

Though Taylor left her suite only for special events, including a dinner in her honor and a press conference kicking off a retrospective of her films, reports of her doings regularly swept the hotel: she's sleeping fitfully; she's napping regularly; she spent two hours on her *maquillage;*

she has food poisoning from spoiled mayonnaise; the food poisoning has made her so ill she's thrown her back out again. At the press conference, she wasn't particularly forthcoming, but did respond to the question: "Are you a feminist?" with "I guess I'm pretty feminine, so I guess I'm pretty feminist. I enjoy being a woman, but I don't feel the necessity to burn bras."

I was so busy recording all these momentous details and relaying them to the office in New York that my hair was unattended, my *maquillage* was nonexistent and my hands were a wasteland of broken fingernails.

There are prices to be paid by foreign correspondents. For some reporters, a foreign assignment means a posting to a war-torn capital. There may be bombings, kidnappings and less than adequate accommodations. For a gossip columnist, a foreign assignment can be equally arduous, except the hotels are usually four-star, and the bombs are restricted mostly to screening rooms at film festivals.

Though I hit any number of parties on the job in New York, most of my working days are spent before a computer terminal, with a phone permanently affixed to my ear. Covering an out-of-town event gives me the opportunity to get out there on the battlefields of gossip, gathering the news stories where they actually occur. Foreign road trips are the most action-packed. I don't view the Academy Awards as foreign—perhaps because I know the turf. Also, most of the people I deal with at the Oscars are New Yorkers, or bicoastal. The sun aside, it's familiar terrain. For a road trip to be foreign, it has to be truly *étranger,* and so completely removed from reality that the locale might as well be another planet.

The year Liz Taylor visited Deauville was my third trip there for the festival of American film, an unusual event, as film festivals go. There are no prizes doled out, as there are at such movie conventions as Cannes, Venice and Berlin, with the exception of an award to a writer selected by Deauville's festival committee. One year it was Gore Vidal, another, Elie Wiesel. Why a writer, I asked Ruda Dauphin, the festival's American organizer? "Because they are French and they are not logical," she replied.

Though some of the films on display at the festival are new to both Americans and Europeans, the majority are U.S. studio releases about to debut on the Continent, but already familiar to American audiences. As a result, on my trips to Deauville, I'd seen most of the movies and didn't spend much time in the festival's theaters.

I didn't choose Deauville, and probably could have gone to Cannes instead, but when I first received an invitation, the timing was right and so I went.

Deauville ended up working out very well for me in terms of making contacts in the film business, and in picking up gossip column items. Because the festival revolves around the stars to whom it stages "homages" or tributes, its focus is more social than business, although there are a fair number of studio executives and marketing men on hand to assure a proper French bow for their films.

Some of the personalities, like Liz Taylor and Dustin Hoffman, who traveled to the festival the same year as Taylor, are bona fide big names. Others are faded luminaries who haven't been seen on the screen in years.

The first year I attended, in 1983, Arlene Dahl was the subject of a film tribute. "Name an Arlene Dahl film" was a favorite game at the bar of the Hotel Royal, the festival's social and gossip center. The organizing committee unearthed a few, including the 1956 Dahl vehicle *Slightly Scarlet,* chosen to launch Dahl's retrospective. The actress would have preferred another of her screen incarnations to have been selected. She was not happy, she said, with the *Slightly Scarlet* image. "I play a nymphomaniac and a kleptomaniac," she explained.

Most of my working hours were spent hanging out at the luxury hotels housing the celebrity visitors, at parties thrown by one or another of the movie studios or at local restaurants frequented by the same Hollywood invaders. Okay, so it wasn't hard labor—but it nonetheless could be tricky figuring out which occurrences qualified as items. I might find it amusing that Shelley Winters had ordered room service, and then greeted the waiter in her birthday suit, but was it hard news?

Well, Deauville wasn't Beirut. I filed what could be considered stock film festival items—which of the American stars were causing riots, and which were being ignored—and I also kept an eye out for controversy.

When Ryan O'Neal, accompanied by Farrah Fawcett, came to Deauville with *Irreconcilable Differences,* he was sporting a black eye. I got all excited, hoping Farrah had whacked him with her purse. No such luck. An amateur pugilist, O'Neal had picked up the shiner sparring at a gym in Paris. It wasn't quite as dramatic as a domestic disturbance, but a story nonetheless.

If festival activities were proving less than active, I would schedule interviews with the actors and directors on hand for the French openings of their films. Even going out to dinner qualified as column material.

One year, I sat at one end of a long, rowdy table at Les Vapeurs, a noisy bistro in nearby Trouville. Elaine Kaufman, who owns Elaine's in New York, was also part of the group, as were actor James Coburn, director Alan Rudolph and director Robert Altman with his sons Bob and Steve.

A magnum of Moët appeared. A diner seated elsewhere in the restaurant volunteered to uncork it, with a saber. His methods left something to be desired, and glass flew across the room, one piece hitting Steve Altman right above the eye. The eatery's waitresses doctored the injury as the champagne started flowing, and flowing. At the end of the evening, with bottles of bubbly adorning most of the tables, everybody stood for a toast, and then tossed their glasses. Elaine was unfazed when hers landed on the bald head of a Frenchman at another table.

Of course, a riot would have made better material, but what with the injury—there had been some blood, after all—and the piles of shattered glass, there was still a story to be had.

If parties, dinners and interviews failed to provide enough material, I had another option for item-hunting— the casino.

Before traveling to Deauville, my casino experience had been limited to a single visit to Atlantic City, which did not prepare me for the grandeur of a French gaming hall.

The croupiers, and most of the patrons, wear evening dress. The subdued atmosphere is drawn from the genteel hush of what is ostensibly old money, diametrically opposed to the clatter of the *nouveau riche* in places like Atlantic City.

Most of the stars associated with films in the festival stop in, as do others who happen to be visiting the resort. One night, Louis Malle and Candice Bergen wandered from table to table. Later, I watched Omar Sharif, who once ran the casino in neighboring Trouville, stare down the baccarat dealers.

On another visit, Ryan O'Neal walked into the casino's bar accompanied by someone who appeared to be a studio executive. Waving his arms, O'Neal was obviously in the middle of an important discussion. "But I can't act," he declared. "I can't act." I didn't hear his companion's response.

Producer Jerry Weintraub, at the festival with *The Karate Kid,* approached Frank Yablans, then the head of MGM, in the same bar. They embraced. Said a producer sitting next to me: "They're both carrying knives. It's what's known as the Hollywood Hug."

Keeping up with Deauville's evening activities meant missing many of the festival's morning programs, press conferences and the like, but it didn't seem to make any difference. There were so many people floating around with no apparent purpose at all that even if I filed only a few stories, I felt like a regular workhorse.

One aspect of Deauville that early on appealed to me was its distance from New York. I was a journalist covering the festival. There were lots of journalists covering the festival. Nobody said: "You write what? Isn't that a GOSSIP column?"

Even when asked to explain myself, I didn't encounter fear and loathing. The first year I attended the festival, I met a producer from London named Michael White. He was curious about my occupation. I explained that I wrote this column for this paper in New York. He'd heard of it.

"So you're the female Nigel Dempster, is that it?" he asked.

I raised an eyebrow: "Do I look like Nigel Dempster?"

He paused, then concluded: "No, you have more hair."

The fact that Deauville was not a part of the real world was most apparent the last time I went there, in 1986, a year marked in France by terrorist attacks. Several of the American stars due at the festival canceled, fearing an event honoring the United States' film industry a likely terrorist target. Armed guards patrolled the streets outside the hotels, but their presence was the only intrusion of reality—and for all the festival-goers knew, the guards might have been there to keep an eye on the rocks in the local Cartier's. I kept forgetting to buy the *International Herald Tribune,* and the terrorists sort of slipped my mind until after the festival, when I traveled to Paris and three bombings in a four-day period.

Rifle-wielding security guards were exceptions to a general Deauville rule dictating that everything and everyone remain genial and pleasant. The unpleasant were to be ignored. "I can't believe I'm getting paid for this" is a thought that more than once crossed my mind.

In the middle of another assignment that proved to be more than foreign, I didn't ask myself that question, feeling quite certain I was earning every cent of my salary.

By the time the New York Giants made it to the football finals in 1987, I was writing the "Inside New York" gossip column for *Newsday.* A huge staff was dispatched to cover the Super Bowl, and its surrounding events. Asked if I wanted to fly to Los Angeles and write the column from there, I saw no point in arguing with a respite from a New York winter.

In retrospect, considering the fact that my beat was Liz, not Lawrence Taylor, I probably should have declined, but once I'd said yes, it was a done deal.

Experience should make gossip easier to gather, but this was an entirely new cast of column characters. I didn't know any of the players, and I don't mean just the guys on the field. It made no difference that they were all from New York. I didn't know any of the owners. I didn't know any of the sportscasters. Jack Kemp put in an appearance to raise money for his presidential race, but I'd only heard of him because he'd switched careers.

Instructed to file a Super Bowl column the day I was traveling to L.A., I was nervous about having time to dig up material when I got there, so I stashed away a couple of emergency stories before leaving. They were extremely lame, I'll admit—but better than nothing.

A friend of mine who'd been a foreign correspondent of the more conventional variety for the New York *Times* had no sympathy for my plight: "As Abe Rosenthal used to say: hit the ground running."

On the plane I frantically looked around for stories. Billy Dee Williams was sitting in first class. He was wearing a Mets jacket. Waste not, it became a mini-item:

"Billy Dee Williams made clear his sports proclivity on a TWA flight en route to Super Bowl-mad L.A. yesterday. The actor sported a blue silk Mets jacket."

Once I settled in at the Beverly Wilshire Hotel, I hit the phones. One call yielded information on Michael J. Fox. Though this was not precisely tied to the pigskin parade, I hated to toss a screen scoop:

"Michael J. Fox is thinking New York this week—but not New York football. Our Hollywood sources, those not afflicted with Super Bowl fever, tell us the 'Back to the Future' star just signed to headline United Artists' film version of Jay McInerney's 'Bright Lights, Big City.' Joyce Chopra will direct."

Even in cases where I had sources, it didn't help much. I would be given information involving people whose identities were a mystery to me, like the owners of the Giants. Befuddled, I would ask the source to repeat the details. Several sources dried up permanently during the trip.

My real incompetence emerged at parties. At one event

I was supposed to be covering, in a hotel ballroom, I noted only two familiar faces: Andy Rooney of "60 Minutes" and sports artist LeRoy Neiman, whose mustache gave him away.

After gathering quotes from them, I approached a man whose blazer was decorated with an NFL patch. Because the event had been advertised as an NFL Alumni banquet, I figured comments from a couple of former gridiron greats would be appropriate.

"Excuse me," I said. "Can you point out a few of the old football stars?"

"Well," he responded. "You just walked right by Ollie Matson."

"Who's Ollie Matson?" I asked.

"WHO's Ollie Matson? WHO's Ollie Matson? He's only one of the greatest ever! He's only in the Hall of Fame! Who's Ollie Matson? I don't believe this."

I slunk away as inobtrusively as possible, and never did have the opportunity to strike up a meaningful conversation with Matson or any other Hall of Famer.

After a day or two of fumbling, I hooked up with Fred Schruers, a New York writer covering the Super Bowl for *Sport* magazine. I told him my tale of woe, of how I had to unearth some stories or I'd be in deep, deep trouble, and he agreed to take me along to a couple of football parties.

A few nights before the game, we drove to Lido Isle for what had been billed as a quarterbacks' party. It was to be held on the second floor of a bank, not the average party site, but what did I know? Maybe football parties had a different set of rules.

I wasn't expecting to recognize anyone, and didn't. Neither did Schruers. There were many tall and wide people in the room, but he couldn't say, definitively, that any were quarterbacks. Joe Namath, the only quarterback I would have recognized, was not there.

As we dissected the landscape, on the verge of regretting the drive from Los Angeles, a familiar face presented itself: Marla Hanson, the fashion model who'd been getting front-page coverage in New York ever since the night she was brutally attacked on a city street. The tabloids often referred to her as "slashed model, Marla Hanson."

We were mystified as to Hanson's presence, but not by the identity of the unctuous-looking individual accompanying her.

"How much you want to bet he's her agent?" I asked.

"That's not a wager," Schruers responded. "It's a given."

Okay, so we definitely had an item here, but a couple of elements were missing, including an explanation as to what Marla Hanson, Slashed Model, was doing at a Super Bowl quarterbacks' party on the second floor of a savings and loan on Lido Isle.

I suggested Schruers go up and ask her. He thought I should do the honors. We couldn't come to a compromise.

"If our editors could see us, we'd both be in big trouble," he predicted.

I tend to avoid parties to which my superiors also have been invited. If any were to see me in action at a social event, I would have been transferred to obituaries a long time ago.

A coin was tossed. Schruers went to get two more beers, and I approached Hanson for the question-and-answer. She said she was in California for rest and relaxation. It wasn't one of your more exciting party interviews.

The next day, virtually on the verge of getting the hang of sports reporting, I was told to drive from Beverly Hills to Anaheim, where the press was headquartered, to pick up credentials for several events, including the Super Bowl itself. I arrived alive, but just barely, and decided to take only the pass needed for the NFL party that night. They could keep the game ticket. If the ride to Anaheim had been that horrendous, I would skip the trip to Pasadena on Sunday, thank you very much.

Traditionally held the Friday night before the Super Bowl, the NFL party is the biggest blowout of the weekend.

Hundreds attend, maybe even thousands. (I'm not great with crowd counts.) Either way, a spacious site is mandatory. In 1987, the NFL took over Lot Z at Universal Studios, and there, in a series of huge tents, put on a display of such tasteless excess that even Liberace would have been appalled.

The entertainment was eclectic. There were belly dancers. There were mimes. A Shirley Temple look-alike tap-danced. A Clark Gable look-alike didn't do anything, other than appear embalmed. The theme of the party was supposed to be—such imagination!—"Hooray for Hollywood." The real theme was "Glitz and Gorge." Most of the guests were overdressed and soon-to-be overfed. The refreshments included shellfish, chili, pastrami, sushi, spareribs, brownies, ice cream and cookies. And that, believe me, was just for starters. I overheard one woman, whose stunning ensemble included a sequined lime green bolero jacket, exclaim: "Hell, I wanna taste of everything!"

Just drinking in the atmosphere was enough for me.

Unfortunately, I was also supposed to be consuming a few stories, but there didn't appear to be any celebrities on hand, none of the big names that had been advertised.

Fred Schruers, who once again had agreed to serve as football party guide, pointed out that there were indeed a few famous people present, but they had all slipped into a roped-off area. Special passes were needed for admission.

"See," he said, "there goes Roger Staubach."

Never have I been so elated. Really, I nearly dropped my soft drink. You see, I had heard of Roger Staubach. Don't ask me where, or why, or how, but I knew his name and the fact that it was connected to football. Tiny tears of joy welled up in my eyes. But, what with the emotional impact of this stunning breakthrough, I didn't feel up to tackling Staubach for a quote.

"I did Marla Hanson," I told Schruers. "It's your turn."

While he was quizzing Staubach, I jotted down a few notes on the overwhelming surroundings. A fellow partygoer approached.

"I'm from Minnesota!" she said, with no little enthusiasm. "Who are you writing for? Where can I read about this?"

Feeling an urge to tell her to try and experience it, rather than wait for the instant replay, I suppressed it, cognizant of her dilemma. It was too darned much to absorb at once. Better to read about it—or watch it on TV.

The lady from Minnesota, who took out her own pen and paper to write down the name of the newspaper for which I worked, was wearing very unusual eyeglasses, featuring a double rim at the edge of the frame—the effect being that of two pair of spectacles worn one on top of the other.

Schruers returned, and also received a request for the name of the publication for which he was writing. As the lady from Minnesota walked away, with a perky "Bye-

bye!" I wondered aloud if she really intended to try and find copies of all the out-of-town newspapers.

"She must read a lot," I surmised.

"Two pair of glasses would indicate a reader," said Schruers.

"Don't be sarcastic, Fred. She was friendly. She was real. She was a football fan."

"Let's go watch people get sick on desserts," he suggested.

Earlier that day, and the day before, I'd been in touch by phone with Michael Fleming and Karen Freifeld, the two reporters who worked with me on the "Inside New York" column. They were gathering East Coast Super Bowl stories while I was working on West.

"What time will you have to leave to get to the game?" Fleming asked.

"I'm not going to the game," I said. "There's some celebrity Super Bowl party at Chasen's. It's right near my hotel. I'll file a story from there."

He was stunned: "You're not going to the game? I can't believe you're not going to the game. What are you doing with your ticket?"

I advised him to keep his voice down or he wouldn't be getting his Super Bowl T-shirt, never mind his embossed Giants bumper sticker.

The next morning, with an entire day before me—and only three or four items to write—I went shopping.

Even in New York, I lack a sense of direction, but it's simpler there. When somebody says "above Fifty-ninth Street," I know they mean Sixtieth, and then Sixty-first. In Los Angeles, directions are very confusing: "East on Sunset" or "West on Santa Monica." What are you supposed to be, a human compass?

The only place I can get to without a map or explicit stoplight-by-stoplight instructions is the Beverly Center. My rental car drives right out of the hotel and propels itself straight to the Beverly Center's multilevel parking without coaxing or directions.

The year of the Super Bowl, it was an oasis of sanity, peopled by individuals uninterested in touchdowns or field goals. Their interests lay in more compelling matters: The brown leather bag, or the black? Pumps, or flats? The cotton knit dress, or the sportswear separates?

When I returned to the hotel, there were several phone messages slipped under the door to my room. Three were from the *Newsday* Super Bowl headquarters in Anaheim, and two from the *Newsday* copy desk in New York.

The number of work-related messages indicated something was up. I fervently hoped my presence was not suddenly required at the Rose Bowl the next day. What if the reporter assigned to writing about tailgate parties had fallen ill and I was being summoned to replace her? I already had begged off that one. I didn't want to write about tailgate parties. I loathe potato salad, and feel even less charitable about parking lots, particularly parking lots filled with inebriated football fans, several of whom assuredly would spill things on me, or subject me to various football-related indignities. But, if duty called, I knew I would be forced to trudge from tailgate to tailgate, collecting insightful quotes like "The Giants are the best" and "I love to party." The story would lead with something innovative, perhaps "Giants fans partied their tails off yesterday . . ."

When I called the office in Anaheim, a harried desk assistant wanted to know where my copy was. I said I would get it in by six, which had been my deadline.

"Haven't you heard? They moved up the edition times. Your copy was due five minutes ago. We've been calling you all day. Where have you been?"

I hid the Ann Taylor bag under the bed.

"How much time did you say I had?"

"No time. Maybe fifteen minutes, at the most. You better send it right out."

Something had happened in the Persian Gulf, or maybe it was Iran, and it was the sort of news you tend to ignore when you are covering the Super Bowl and are only reading the sections of the newspaper that directly pertain to The Big Event. Whatever it was, and wherever it had taken place, it had pushed up the edition times and my copy was due several hours earlier than it had been the day before.

If all I had to do was write, it wouldn't have been so bad, but I'd strolled casually into my hotel room, confident in the knowledge that I had a few hours to make a couple of fact-checking phone calls, and then dash off my stories.

Calls were placed. People who were supposed to check facts did not pick up phones. I eliminated said potential facts from stories and hurriedly strung together the information I had.

Then I tried using the computerized phone hook-up to transmit the copy. It didn't work a first, a second or a third time. In between failed attempts, I received additional phone calls from the copy desk demanding my material. If the Persian Gulf exploded, I wondered, would anyone care that three middle-aged women had expressed undying love for Andy Rooney in a hotel ballroom, that Johnny Carson had been to a party for Pete Rozelle, or that Marla Hanson, Slashed Model, had virtually nothing to say when questioned on the second floor of a savings and loan on Lido Isle? Actually, I knew the answer. They would skip the Persian Gulf and read only about the Super Bowl.

After several more attempts, and a couple of futile recitations of the Act of Contrition, I surrendered. The computer hook-up did not work. I would have to dictate. The copy desk sounded a tad peeved when I relayed this information. Super Bowl coverage was proving exhausting, and I would need a nap when it was over.

The next day, slightly comatose from football activities, I prepared for the celebrity party at Chasen's in Beverly Hills, thinking as I did how pleasant it would be if the action to be observed there would happen fast, and early. I gave it about an hour, jotting down celebrity names— Rodney Dangerfield, Bob Newhart, Gene Kelly, Norman Lear—and picking up a couple of quotes. Then I filed a story from a phone in the restaurant's ladies' room. Lucie Arnaz, Shirlee Fonda and assorted other female guests gave me strange looks as they trooped by to use the facilities. I congratulated myself for remembering the spellings of both "Lucie" and, especially, "Shirlee." When you've been doing this sort of thing for a while, important details tend to linger. The lead on the story was:

"Why shlep to Pasadena for the Super Bowl when you can park it comfortably at Chasen's?"

It made sense to me. I went back to the hotel before the game had even started and slept for the rest of the afternoon. Later, I learned the Giants had won.

I am offended by remarks about the facile nature of the gossip profession: what a cushy job; it must be so much fun; all the great parties you go to, and the interesting people, and the fascinating places.

211

Foreign gossip correspondence is a very serious business.

Will Liz Taylor's back hold out? Does Yves Montand intend to show up for the opening gala? Why isn't Sigourney Weaver talking to American reporters?

If O. J. Simpson speaks at the Jack Kemp fundraiser, does that mean he's a Republican? What is Joe DiMaggio doing here? Is he a Republican too? And what about Frank Gifford's wife? Will she ever stop smiling?

She never did—not in public, anyway. I guess no one told her about the Persian Gulf.

Chapter 11

TRUMP AND BESS IN SCOOP MESS

Certain gossip columnists leave readers no doubt about the importance of certain items. They trumpet them with a one-word introduction: "Scoop!"

What makes a scoop is purely a matter of opinion, in my opinion. One columnist's column-leading scoop is another's filler of the odd empty space.

Take Kevin Costner being cast as Eliot Ness in the film version of "The Untouchables." I got the information from a source in Hollywood, and wrote it up as a brief casting note in the middle of a column led off by another story of presumably more importance. The casting choice was interesting, and the movie in advance looked like a winner. But, who ever knows, before the cameras roll, if a hit or a star is in the making? Not me, that's for sure. There are too many variables. Still, I thought Costner being named to play Ness might have some reader interest.

It must have had a lot because in the six or so months that followed, I observed the "Costner to Play Ness!" story pop up all over the place, including at least two other gossip columns. In each case, the story was heralded as a major movie scoop.

Each time I saw yet another repetition of the story, I thought perhaps I was burdened with poor news judgment. In light of the film's subsequent success, I guess I should have played it up much bigger. But the movie could have fallen flat on its financial and critical faces, in which case I would have stashed my connection to the illuminating information under the nearest bushel.

Certain scoops don't need introductions as such. The sheer weight of the material makes its own impact.

When Sean Penn and Madonna decided to marry, Suzy, then with the *Daily News,* broke the story. More than one editor at the *Post* hovered over my desk that day to chide me for missing such an important item. I reminded them that I had been first with news of the romance itself, but no one seemed to care. That was yesterday's hot story.

Because the Madonna–Sean Penn story was acted upon immediately by the wire services and other news organizations, there was no chance the news would spring up six months later—bannered "Exclusive!"—as had happened in the case of the Costner/Ness story, without anyone remembering that it had already appeared in print.

Many scoops melt away with such rapidity, their impact is questionable at best. One day there is no story any bigger, no news more important. The next, there's another column to fill, and what have you done for me lately?

In the case of the Bess Mess, as it came to be called, there was no way of knowing that a 1983 Page Six story about Bess Myerson's perhaps coincidental hand in the hiring of a woman whose mother, a state supreme court judge, was presiding over the divorce of Myerson's boyfriend, was a scoop. The story was several years old before anyone really paid any attention to it. Any overt attention, that is.

The attention level has risen considerably, and last October, Myerson was indicted by a federal grand jury on charges that included conspiracy, mail fraud and obstruction of justice. Myerson's beau, Queens contractor Carl "Andy" Capasso (already serving jail time for tax fraud) and former State Supreme Court Justice Hortense Gabel were named in the same indictment, charging that they conspired to reduce Capasso's temporary alimony by having Myerson hire the judge's daughter. As the divorce-fixing conspiracy case developed, Bess Myerson continued to declare her innocence. "The reason this is happening," she once stated. "Is that I'm a woman. I'm a Miss America. I'm Queen of the Jews."

No column—no newspaper, for that matter—is as important as the people writing or editing it might like to think it is. It provides information, some good, some bad, and yes, there are people who read and are influenced by a specific story, or scoop. But for each person so influenced, there are a dozen more who never see the news item and wouldn't care if they did.

That is not to say columns and newspapers don't have an impact. All you have to do is watch what happens when the New York *Times* affixes a three- or four-star rating to a restaurant to know that newspapers make a difference. They can ruin a nice restaurant overnight.

A story is written and runs in the paper, and that, quite often, is the end of it. Or so it seems. But sometimes things aren't as they seem—and appearances are altered to soften the blow of a news story, which I suppose backs up the theory that newspapers make an impact. The story of Bess Myerson and Sukhreet Gabel was not at all what it seemed. It certainly made an impact.

In the spring and summer of 1983, I ran a couple of

stories about Bess Myerson, the former Miss America and at that point New York City's Cultural Affairs Commissioner, and her boyfriend Andy Capasso. Capasso was in the process of divorcing his wife Nancy. It was a messy situation.

So was a tip I received about a woman Myerson had hired to work for her, Sukhreet Gabel. Wasn't it interesting, the source noted, that Gabel's mother just happened to be the judge presiding over the divorce of Andy and Nancy Capasso? It was no coincidence, said the source.

A story appeared in the lead space on Page Six, on October 18, 1983, under the headline: "Small world: Bess hires kin of divorce judge." It almost didn't run as a lead, because of the emphatic denials of any conflict of interest. Richard Johnson, the Page Six reporter who did the legwork on the story, ran into resistance at every turn.

Said Justice Gabel: "I didn't even know Bess Myerson was involved in this [divorce case] until I saw a piece on Page Six a few weeks ago."

Sukhreet Gabel said she didn't know anything about her mother's cases or her boss's social life, except for what she read in the papers.

Richard Bruno, who also worked for Bess Myerson, said he, not Myerson, had interviewed, then hired Sukhreet Gabel.

Though the denials were strong, the coincidence of Justice Gabel's daughter working for Myerson was enough to make a story. But was it enough for a lead story? In retrospect, it was enough for the front page of the paper.

The item appeared, and caused some comment, although not an unusual amount. Not that I was aware of, in any case. There was a lot of comment I wouldn't be aware of until nearly four years later, when the Page Six story would be cited in an investigative report on Myerson, in which she would be accused of "serious misconduct."

In the report, commissioned by New York's Mayor Ed Koch, Harold Tyler, a former federal judge who compiled the findings, noted the existence of a "secret understanding" between Myerson and Justice Hortense Gabel. The understanding involved Myerson hiring Sukhreet Gabel to work as her special assistant. Two weeks after Sukhreet Gabel started her city job, her mother reduced the alimony and child support to be paid by Myerson's boyfriend.

The report also told of Myerson's wooing Sukhreet Gabel, described in the report by her father as "emotionally disturbed," by taking her to dinner and having intimate, motherly chats with her.

When the New York *Times* wrote about the Tyler report in June of 1987 it stated: "After a small item about the hiring of the judge's daughter appeared in the New York Post in October 1983, Ms. Myerson wrote a letter to Mr. Koch in which she asserted that a subordinate had suggested hiring Ms. Gabel, that Ms. Gabel was superior to other candidates and that Justice Gabel had already made the major decisions in the divorce case by the time her daughter was hired." According to Tyler, this letter, prompted by the Page Six story, was "a deception."

Boy, was I ever insulted. The lead story on Page Six was hardly a "small item," when you consider the fact that it's the main piece on the most widely read page in the *Post.* Also, the *Times* dismissed the Page Six piece as a "small item" in the middle of a front-page story about the Tyler report, which acknowledged the Page Six story as the first to publicly bring out the "coincidence" of Myerson's hiring Sukhreet Gabel.

Here is how Tyler referred to the Page Six piece in his report: "Although the news story accurately reported the essential facts that Ms. Gabel was employed at the [Department of Cultural Affairs] and that her mother was presiding over the Capasso divorce, the story substantially understated the relationship between the parties." But, Tyler noted, the understatement wasn't really Page Six's fault: "It did so as the result of false information given the newspaper by Sukhreet Gabel and by a D.C.A. assistant commissioner acting at Ms. Myerson's direction."

Another section of the report states that: "The hiring of Sukhreet Gabel remained quiet for the next few years. After publication of the Post story, however, Ms. Gabel's relationship with Ms. Myerson immediately deteriorated and Ms. Myerson had little to do with her thereafter."

I wasn't aware any of this was going on at City Hall. I didn't know about a letter to Ed Koch from Bess Myerson, or of the disintegration of any relationship between Myerson and Sukhreet Gabel. The story died, and I didn't think about it again until U.S. Attorney Rudolph Giuliani began investigating Andy Capasso, whose firm held lucrative contracts with New York City. When called to testify, Bess Myerson pleaded the Fifth Amendment before a federal grand jury, much to the chagrin of Mayor Koch. In the midst of a plague of scandals, he had said he'd dismiss any official of his government who refused to testify before a grand jury.

After Myerson's pleading the Fifth became public, she took an unpaid leave of absence from her city job, and eventually resigned. Harold Tyler began putting together his report, the contents of which Giuliani and Mayor

Koch ordered be kept secret, citing possible interference in the ongoing Capasso investigation. It was until *The Village Voice* got its hands on it in June of 1987.

I guess I should have been faulted for not following up immediately on the original story, but in light of the denials, and the fact that Justice Gabel went to Nancy Capasso's attorney Raoul Felder after the story appeared and asked him if he felt she should remove herself from the case, and he said no, there didn't seem to be a clear follow-up.

Also, stories involving divorces, and corespondents in divorce cases, are inherently sticky. If the stories emanated, as some of them did, from an impartial court reporter who happened upon the information, that was one thing. But many of them came from sources who had large and unwieldy axes to grind. That certainly didn't invalidate the information, but it meant additional scrutiny was required before running the story.

After the Myerson-Gabel story appeared on Page Six, it seemed like it might have been just a coincidence. Everybody said it was a coincidence, and if it was, wasn't it sort of unfair to keep badgering these people? I wish I'd badgered.

The one aspect of the unfolding of the Bess Mess that I found amusing—if that adjective can be used to describe anything in a situation so disastrous—was the delicacy with which Tyler and the New York *Times* at first side-stepped around the fact that the original story had appeared in a GOSSIP COLUMN. Instead, it was "a small item" or a "story in the New York Post." They couldn't quite bring themselves to actually use the dread term. Really, sniff, it's so distasteful—and an essential truth of journalism. When you pursue a story like this for a gossip column in the New York *Post,* you're a sleazy purveyor of the sordid and sensational. When you do it for the New York *Times,* you're an investigative reporter.

The Myerson/Gabel story was a scoop scored, but it could have been a scoop missed if the denials had been heeded, and the story discarded. No matter how well wired a gossip columnist is, there are those who will try to snip those wires—cutting away potential scoops, by denying stories.

Of all the wire cutters I've encountered, Donald Trump carries the sharpest instruments.

Trump, the wealthy and influential real estate developer, wasn't as public a figure as he is now when I first encountered him. On some level, sorry to say, I've helped contribute to his profile by writing about him frequently, but he is so outrageous as to be irresistible gossip column copy.

Trump is not blind to the fact that he is appealing to the media, and he doesn't try to avoid phone calls from reporters. I've always appreciated the easy access—not that it has ever made getting the right angle on a Trump story any easier.

"I don't know anything about it" is Trump's favorite phrase. He's a busy guy. He's an important guy. He's usually right in the thick of things, but more often than not, when I've called his office to check on something in which he is involved, he doesn't know anything about it. I guess certain things just slip his mind. You know how it is when you're busy.

The fact that Trump's memory has problematic properties doesn't keep me from writing certain stories, but it makes it harder to know how to play them.

Take Lincoln West. I certainly didn't know how to play that story.

In March of 1983, I had received a tip about Trump's involvement in Lincoln West, a seventy-six-acre site running alongside the Hudson River from Fifty-ninth to Seventy-second streets, upon which a $1 billion commercial and residential complex was to be built. Trump, my source informed me, was discussing investing in the project, and might even buy out developer Abe Hirschfeld and others involved in the proposed complex. When the Trump development developed, I was told, it would be a very big deal.

When I asked him about this, Trump responded that he was "absolutely not" involved in Lincoln West in any way, and was not even talking to anyone about it. I didn't run the story immediately, but my source kept after me.

"When are you going to run the Lincoln West story?"

"Trump denies it."

"It's true, I'm telling you."

"But I don't have any confirmation at all. And Abe Hirschfeld won't talk to me."

"Doesn't that tell you something?"

Yes, it did tell me something. I made more calls, and finally got somebody else to tell me, off-the-record, that Trump was talking to the Lincoln West people. As I pressed a little harder for something on-the-record, my source pressed me.

"This is an unbelievably great story," said the source, stressing that the land involved was the biggest undeveloped piece of property in Manhattan.

"If you don't run something," said the source, "I really should leak it to somebody else."

On April 7, I finally ran a piece on Lincoln West, accompanied by Trump's denial. My source was not happy.

"You didn't run it as a lead! You pissed it away as an item."

"Well, I didn't have much to go on."

"Unbelievable. Remind me not to give you any more great stories."

Not long after this, I came across information about Trump buying a palatial country home in Connecticut. This time, he didn't get on the phone himself, but had a spokesperson deny, several times, not only that he was purchasing said home, but he also denied that his wife Ivana was overseeing the decorating of the place. Page Six finally ran the story, with no comment from Trump. He now spends weekends in the house, parts of which were decorated by his wife Ivana.

The next time Page Six called Trump, I wanted to find out about a three-hour meeting Trump had had in his office with Richard Nixon. The same spokesperson said Trump knew nothing about such a meeting. Said Richard Nixon's aide Nick Ruwe: "He went to Donald Trump's office about 10:30 A.M. . . . It was a private meeting." Though Nixon has had a few problems with credibility in his time, I went with his aide's version of the meeting.

The Lincoln West story became bigger and bigger news. It's still big news. Trump's feud with Mayor Ed Koch over Lincoln West, now known as the site of Trump's proposed, and consistently controversial, Television City development, had formed the basis of several recent front-page stories. I suppose I should be happy that I wrote about it before anybody else did, but, actually, I completely blew one of the major Lincoln West news scoops.

About eighteen months after our original story on Lincoln West, Page Six reporter Richard Johnson scheduled an interview with Trump at his office in Trump Tower. The developer had announced that he would be willing to help President Reagan in arms negotiations with the Soviet Union. Trump had declared himself not only willing, but eminently able; his business was deals, he said. The focus of Johnson's interview was to be the proposed arms negotiations, which I thought would make an interesting story.

The day before the interview, when Johnson was confirming the time and other details, Trump suggested I accompany Johnson. He said he'd never met me. Well, that wasn't quite true. I'd been introduced to him two or three times at social events, but why quibble about details?

So Johnson and I went up to Trump Tower on Friday morning, November 30, 1984. We waited a few minutes while Trump was finishing up other business and then he ushered us into his extremely spacious quarters, with views of the city so expansive I was momentarily speechless.

Only for a moment, though. Trump told us he liked the New York *Post,* and he was delighted to talk with us. Not that he paid much attention to press, he said. He didn't think it was all that important. Then he opened a desk drawer and pulled out a couple of copies of a profile of him that had appeared in the Washington *Post.* Had we seen it, he wondered?

Johnson asked lots of questions about arms negotiations. I asked lots of questions about Lincoln West.

At that point, several other news reports on the West Side development had appeared, and Trump reportedly was quite close to finalizing arrangements to buy the Lincoln West site. I was polite in asking the questions, figuring that would be the best way to present the issue. It didn't work.

Nothing was really happening right then with Lincoln West, Trump told us, pointing to a map of the property he had on the floor. Something might soon, he said, and he'd let us know when it did, but not a thing was going on right then.

We finished our chat, jumped in a cab and returned to the *Post*. As it was Friday, we had two columns to complete that day and were rushed. I'd already written one lead, about the Mobil Oil Company boycotting *The Wall Street Journal*, for Monday, and Richard had a lead about Geraldine Ferraro hitting the lecture circuit for Saturday. I told him to hang on to the Trump interview until Monday and we'd run it on Tuesday. Trump certainly hadn't talked to anyone else about arms negotiations that day, so the story would hold. I left the office in a very cheerful mood. Here it was Friday afternoon and we already had a lead story backed up for Tuesday. This didn't happen very often.

The next morning, I sat down with a cup of coffee, and the Saturday New York *Times*. On the front page was a story headlined: TRUMP SET TO BUY LINCOLN WEST SITE. The story began: "Donald J. Trump said yesterday that he had an agreement to buy the site of the proposed $1 billion Lincoln West housing and office complex on the West Side and that he planned to redesign the project."

"Said yesterday?" SAID YESTERDAY?

I dreaded going into the office on Monday. Practically the moment I walked in, the phone on my desk rang. It was Roger Wood: "Dear girl, could you come into my office for a moment?"

So I went into Wood's office. He did not look like a happy executive editor.

"Didn't you and Johnson interview Trump on Friday?"

"Uhmm, yeah."

"Then why in the name of god was the Lincoln West story on the front page of the *Times* on Saturday and not the *Post?* Do you realize how foolish this makes us look?"

"Roger, I swear, I asked him about it and he said nothing was happening."

"You didn't ask hard enough, dear girl, because obviously a great deal was happening. I want you to find out why we didn't have this story."

"I intend to."

"Go to it."

So I called Trump. He was busy, his assistant said, and he'd call me back. It was important, I said, and would appreciate it if he got back to me sooner rather than later.

When he called back, he said he'd really enjoyed chatting with me and Richard.

Golly, Mr. Trump, I said, we enjoyed it too, but what was this on the front page of the *Times?* You said nothing was going on with Lincoln West.

Trump apologized, explaining that his hands were tied.

"I had an arrangement with the *Times,"* he said. "I had to give it to them first."

Squelching an urge to jump up and down and bellow into the phone, I said quietly, "You had a what?"

"I had a deal with the *Times.* I was going to call you today and tell you about it."

What's a gossip columnist to do? I don't think he even

realized that denying a story in an interview with one newspaper on the very day you're giving the same story to another newspaper is—how shall I put this?—not done. Not if you want to remain on speaking terms with the newspaper you screwed out of the story. The least he could have done was reschedule the interview. Either he didn't get it, or he got it quite coherently—and didn't really give a damn. Take your pick.

After the *Times* story on Lincoln West ran, I was what you'd call a mite miffed, and told Johnson to bag the arms negotiation interview. I thought Trump had gotten quite enough press that week.

There are numerous evasive ways to get around answering a journalist's questions. There is "no comment." There is: "I don't discuss that sort of thing with reporters." There is: "He's too busy to return calls today." I'm not wild about evasion, but I've learned to live with it.

Once, after a particularly frustrating exchange with Trump, I called his lawyer, Roy Cohn, and asked him if he wouldn't mind giving his client a few lessons in media relations. Cohn found this highly amusing.

"Oh, he doesn't really mean it," Cohn chuckled. "He's just very excitable."

He sure is, which is one of the reasons I continued to write about him. Donald Trump is not only excitable, he's exciting. And, like an elephant in your bathtub, he's very hard to ignore.

There are many more Donald Trump scoops I haven't had: Trump to refurbish Central Park's Wollman Rink; Trump talks to NBC for Television City; Trump buys Resorts International. The one I was really sorry to have missed was: Trump to appear in mini-series.

In a television adaptation of Judith Krantz's *I'll Take*

Manhattan, part of which was to be filmed in the Trump Tower, Trump was signed for a daunting acting assignment—the role of real estate developer Donald Trump. Now that's what I call a screen scoop.

Chapter 12

MENDACIOUS MINION FLEES MUG SHOT

Radie Harris is known in show business for two things: her *Hollywood Reporter* column, "Broadway Ballyhoo," and her artificial leg. She's been writing the column for centuries. I don't know how long she's had the leg.

Not long before Earl Wilson cut back on his output of daily columns for the *Post*, Jim Brady, then editing Page Six, got a call from Radie.

"Earl is too old to keep doing that column," she declared. At the time, Earl was in his mid-seventies. I doubt Radie was much younger.

Radie had a suggestion: "We all know Earl's going to retire anyway. I think I should do that column. Now I know this Rudolph Murdoch and I think he's a fine fellow, but you know him better than I do. I think you should go right in and tell Rudy to hire me to write Earl's column."

Did Brady ever make the suggestion? I have no idea, though I do know that Radie did not replace Earl when he retired. I also know that her phone call painted a new portrait of Rupert Murdoch for me. Tough-as-nails press lord? Heck no. I started to think of him as good old Rudy, a real fine fellow.

Or Uncle Rudy, mysterious, all-knowing and all-powerful, yet friendly and generous, not unlike the avuncular figure behind the curtain in *The Wizard of Oz.* When picking up the check after lunch with a source, I would say, "Please, Uncle Rudy insists."

Murdoch doesn't really have an image. He has images, of variegated hue. The newspaper executives who are his longtime associates are a rowdy and ribald bunch. He's known them all for years, but hardly seems just another "mate." From what I gather, Murdoch is not only politically conservative, but personally as well. I can't quite picture him Limp Falling.

When I started at the *Post,* Murdoch was perceived by the rest of the New York media as a foreign invader. On a *Time* magazine cover that appeared soon after he bought the paper, he was portrayed as King Kong climbing the Empire State Building. Who is this guy, New Yorkers were asking themselves, and what is he after?

He was after a lot, including the *Star* and the *Post,* and *The Village Voice,* and newspapers in Texas, Boston and Chicago. He also over the years has bought up or started a slew of magazines, starting with *New York* and *New West,* and more recently, *New Woman, Elle* and *Premiere.*

The acquisitions didn't end there. Eventually, he bought a group of television stations, a movie studio, 20th Century-Fox, and Harper & Row, the publishing house.

One day during the early part of my *Post* experience, Roger Wood was away and Murdoch came down and ran the city desk himself. As the years went by, he seemed less involved in the day-to-day operation of the paper, but continued to maintain his office in the building housing the *Post,* and would occasionally make the rounds of the fourth-floor editorial quarters. As his American power and possessions grew, and I'd spot him striding through the city room, it wasn't a person I saw, but a walking, multimedia conglomerate.

Several months after I'd left the *Post* and had moved to New York *Newsday,* I went to cover yet another party on the Forbes yacht. At this point in my floating party career, my sea legs were in shape.

While waiting for a drink at the bar, I chatted with the woman standing next to me.

"Isn't it a lovely night for a boat ride?" she said.

I agreed. We exchanged pleasantries, commenting upon one or another of the landmarks in the Manhattan skyline as we passed them by.

"We haven't met," she said. "I'm Anna Murdoch."

"Oh," I said. "I guess I should have known that. I used to work for your husband." I introduced myself.

"I recognize the name," she responded.

A few minutes later, as I was walking to the other end of the boat, I nearly collided with her husband.

"Mr. Murdoch?"

"Yes?" He obviously had no idea who I was.

Again, I introduced myself.

"Oh yes," he said. "And how are you liking *Newsday?*"

I said I liked it just fine. Though it wasn't a particularly memorable conversation, I wish I had it on videotape to show to those, and there were many, who over the years had accused Page Six, and its editor, of being puppets controlled by a manipulative Murdoch.

An item about a lawyer once ran on Page Six, an item the lawyer did not like. He called to complain.

"Murdoch told you to run that story, didn't he?" said the lawyer.

I said he most certainly had not. The lawyer wasn't convinced.

"Who are you kidding?" he said. "Everybody knows he tells you what to write, and who to nail."

Though I don't doubt Murdoch once in a while passed along story ideas to Page Six through other editors, he certainly never called up with any personally while I was there, and I was never told that a particular story HAD to run because Murdoch wanted it in the paper. It was a shame, really. He could have been a great source, if he hadn't been the paper's owner.

In the spring of 1985, in an article in the *Washington Journalism Review,* attorney Floyd Abrams, the First Amendment specialist, said he'd attempted to kick the New York *Post* habit, but was weakening and might have to give in. "Page Six," Abrams was quoted as saying, "is one of the things hardest to give up."

Page Six tended to have that sort of an effect on people, myself included, but even the strongest addictions can be broken. Several months later, after nearly eight years at the *Post,* I thought it might be time for a change. I quit right before Thanksgiving.

On my final day at the column, the staff organized a bon voyage party, during which I was presented with a blown-up photo of my favorite celebrity, C. Fred Bush, complete with personally inscribed paw print. It was a most exciting addition to my collection of celebrity memorabilia.

The final column didn't feature any earth-shattering scoops, though it did contain an interesting story about Henry Kissinger mulling over a run for a Senate seat, and another on Woody Allen shooting a scene for his latest movie in Rockaway. Asked how he would describe the director, a resident of the Queens neighborhood had responded: "He's a little guy in a jacket."

And, when I quit, I found myself in an unusual position —on the other side of the fence as the subject of a gossip item. Liz Smith reported that my post-*Post* plans included contemplation of the question, "Is there life without gossip?"

It was a question I'd mulled over before, at Canyon Ranch, a fat farm in Tucson.

Some time earlier, when the gossip mill had started to wear me down, I made reservations for a week's stay at the Arizona spa. I had many goals to achieve. Quit smoking. Stop drinking. Acquire fashion model's figure. Have massages and facials. It would be a busy week, and at the end I would emerge a new person, a pristine vessel prepared to return to New York and fend off further pollution.

Upon checking in, I was handed a form, which included a list of such evil substances as caffeine, nicotine, alcohol and sugar. Next to each was a little box to be checked according to intake of the evil substance. I checked all the boxes marked "frequently."

I brought a stack of books with me, planning to evolve into a vegetable-like state, far from Australians, far from celebrities, far from gossip. Then I saw Barbra Streisand in yoga class.

It wasn't her fault. She had just as much right to go to a fat farm as I. But couldn't she have gone to some other fat farm?

I was the only guest at Canyon Ranch not thrilled with Streisand's presence. If Barbra Streisand had picked this fat farm, the thinking was, then it must be The Right Fat Farm. As I was exiting the locker room one day, I heard a woman declare: "This leotard was in the same maxi-power class as Barbra Streisand. I'll never wash it again."

Streisand was accompanied by her former agent Sue Mengers, who, according to my fat farm sources, was trying to woo Streisand back into her stable of show biz clients. She wasn't successful, but you couldn't fault her for trying. I don't know if I would have been willing to contort my way through that many yoga classes, or consume that many bran cakes.

Several days after I arrived, I called the Page Six staff back in New York. Everything was fine, I was told. Was I having a nice rest? Sort of, I said, if only Barbra Streisand hadn't appeared. Barbra Streisand? Great, they said, now you can file a Barbra Streisand-goes-to-fat-farm story.

That's the annoying thing about celebrities. Just when you think you've escaped them, one or two will pop up out of nowhere and you're back on the item trail.

I know, or at least hope, that someday I will be in a restaurant somewhere and a very famous movie star will walk in, and when that very famous movie star does, I won't even look up. It won't even occur to me to think: is an item on the horizon?

A friend of mine who worked briefly on a gossip column told me it took a while to restructure her brain waves out of the Item-Think pattern. But, she said, it was possible.

I don't know. She only worked on a column for a year.

The week at the fat farm, despite the Streisand intrusion, did put me in a better frame of mind, and I returned to Page Six determined not to fall back into my bad habits. It worked to some extent, but it didn't mean there was life without gossip.

After leaving the *Post,* I decided I would spend several months working on a book. But then I was approached by Don Forst, the editor of New York *Newsday,* about joining the staff of that paper to edit a Page Six-like column. *Newsday,* part of the Times-Mirror group, had just begun its drive into the New York City market. It might be interesting to be on hand as the presses of a new tabloid started rolling, but did I really want to write another gossip column?

It was tempting. I sort of missed the excitement inherent in the operation of a daily newspaper. Working at home, I wasn't scoring any scoops, and I never heard from any deli flacks.

I started the job in February of 1986.

The column, "Inside New York," appears, appropriately, on page six, and much of its focus is similar to the other Page Six.

But there are differences too.

The column runs five, not six days a week, and the editorial process is considerably more ordered. Also, the office is in midtown. They don't find all that many dead bodies near the building, but you can't have everything.

Most of my sources are those I generated personally, and they followed me to New York *Newsday.* There are also those who called me only because I wrote Page Six, and I haven't heard from them since I left the *Post.* It's no loss as far as I'm concerned. Who needs fairweather sources?

There hasn't been a shortage of scoops, in any case: Sylvester Stallone backs out of the Cannes Film Festival amid threats of terrorism; *Esquire* magazine sold to the Hearst Corporation; Meryl Streep and Jack Nicholson signed to star in *Ironweed;* Philippine government officials to sell contents of Ferdinand and Imelda Marcos' New York townhouse.

One of the more scintillating scoops involved Little Richard's conversion to Judaism: "If you need Little Richard, don't try him [Friday night]. He'll be at *shul.*"

Leaving the *Post* also has opened up a whole new category of items—about the workings of the Murdoch empire.

One of those stories was about Barry Diller, head of Murdoch's Fox, and *Crocodile Dundee.* The movie's star, Paul Hogan, and several other individuals involved in the making of the film, knew Murdoch, and had offered their fellow Australian and his movie studio first crack at U.S. distribution rights to *Dundee.* Diller twice was supposed to screen the film, but never got around to it. The *Dundee* producers finally took their product elsewhere. Paramount picked up American rights to the movie for $3 million. At last count, it has grossed some $130 million in the United States, and there is a sequel on the way, to which Paramount also has U.S. rights.

Now I'm also free to write about Murdoch's publications, including the *Post.*

For several months after I left, Steve Dunleavy functioned as the uncredited overseer of Page Six. When I heard the rumors of his leaving for Channel 5, the local television station Murdoch had purchased, I decided to write a story about it, and called for a comment.

"Rubbish, dear girl," was his response. I ran the story anyway.

Some time later, after he'd moved to Channel 5, I had another story involving him, and a management change at the station. When I called, he wasn't in and I left a message. The next day, an assistant picked up his phone. I identified myself, and she put me on hold.

"He's busy right now," she said. "Would you like to leave a message?"

I went through this charade another time before realizing he had no intention of calling me back. I'd have to think of something else.

The next time I phoned Dunleavy, I told the assistant Sheila Devin was calling.

Sheila Devin was the name used by the Mayflower Madam, Sydney Biddle Barrows, when she was running her New York escort service. Dunleavy took the call.

"Is this what it's come to, Steve?" I asked. "I have to pretend I'm the Mayflower Madam to get you on the phone?"

There was dead air for a moment on the other end of the line, followed by his response:

"Well, you work the same bloody beat, don't you?"

In the mutable microcosm of the media, Dunleavy can be relied upon as a constituent rare in its constancy.

I've never been certain precisely what my beat is, anyway. At both the *Post* and *Newsday*, the scoring of "serious" stories is encouraged, along with those of the "silly ass" bent. At some point, I expect the line between gossip and news to distinguish itself definitively. It hasn't happened yet.

When I interviewed Britain's longest-running gossip act, Nigel Dempster of the *Daily Mail*, for New York *Newsday*, I asked him what he thought of New York's gossip columns.

He declared them "totally at the feet of the people they write about . . . they can't afford to write anything nasty."

I said I didn't agree. He continued:

"If you've got no form of society, you've got no gossip. You've got nothing to write about. You're writing about non-people."

According to Dempster, a gossip item has to be "pejorative. It's got to be something where everyone says 'ha, ha, ha.' The non-appeal. You can't do that in this town because the people are of no consequence . . . The people you're writing about, their only consequence is their credit rating. They've got no style, no class."

In England, Dempster said, "We've got people like Donald Trump, but they're dukes. And they've been around for 350 years, not 350 weeks. And so Donald Trump is just a cheapskate who's put up a tower. But the Duke of Westminster, who's half the age of Donald Trump and five times as rich, is someone who's got lineage."

Dempster also had plenty to say about Murdoch, or at least about the journalists who work for Murdoch's papers in England.

"I call them Murdoch's Mendacious Minions," said Dempster. "They don't have to research stories. They don't have to look for stories. They just lie and they invent."

Gee, I said, I used to work for Murdoch and I was required to check out my stories.

Unfazed, he added: "They're just the worst."

Later I asked him if he ever felt obligated to write about people in whom his readers have some interest, even if he doesn't.

"Of course not," he scoffed. "I write about people only as long as I'm interested in them. I've consigned hundreds of people to the dustbins of history, and when I don't write about them anymore, they don't exist."

Had I missed the point all along? Should I have been trying to sweep people like Donald Trump into dustbins? It was an appealing concept, but, no, I don't think so.

There will always be an England, and New York isn't it.

The gossip columns in New York will never be like those in London, nor will those in New York now be like those here ten years hence. Something else, some other Watergate, will occur, and they'll be altered again. I won't be writing one, but I'll still be reading them, because gossip columns are the dessert of journalism, and I like dessert.

First comes the New York *Times,* and *The Wall Street Journal,* then maybe the Washington *Post* or the Los Angeles *Times,* and then the tabloids, filled with madness, mayhem, murder—and gossip.

The reasons I know I'll be a reader of gossip in ten years, rather than a writer, are many. The "the thrill is gone" factor is one. There are only so many Pia Zadora scoops a columnist can land, when, suddenly, one is hit, and the pulse doesn't race.

The "mug" factor is another. As Evelyn Waugh, author of *Scoop,* the classic novel about Fleet Street, once was said to have remarked: "Anyone who's a reporter after forty is a mug."

"Mug" is a British expression meaning "a person easily deceived"—basically, a sucker. I gather it's even more insulting than "wanker."

Go figure.

ABOUT THE AUTHOR

For three years SUSAN MULCAHY edited the New York *Post*'s gossipy Page Six. She is currently performing similar tasks for New York *Newsday*'s "Inside New York" column. Before graduating from Barnard College in New York, Mulcahy somehow ended up as a copy girl at the *Post.* An assistant's position on Page Six opened up and her career as a celebrity journalist began. Her favorite celebrities are Bishop Tutu, Princess Diana, C. Fred Bush and Mel Gibson.